THE *BEST* BOOK ABOUT
VIRGINIA CAR ACCIDENTS & INJURIES

Essential Information You Should Know *Before* You Hire an Attorney or Talk to the Insurance Company

JOHN COOPER, JIM HURLEY, BILL O'MARA & GRIFFIN M. O'HANLON

COOPER HURLEY INJURY LAWYERS

WORD ASSOCIATION PUBLISHERS
www.wordassociation.com
1.800.827.7903

Printed in the United States of America.

ISBN: 978-1-63385- 312-6

Published by
Word Association Publishers
205 Fifth Avenue
Tarentum, Pennsylvania 15084

www.wordassociation.com
1.800.827.7903

COOPER HURLEY
INJURY LAWYERS

Jim Hurley, ESQ

John Cooper, ESQ

Bill O'Mara, ESQ

Griffin M. O'Hanlon, ESQ

LOCATIONS IN:

NORFOLK, VIRGINIA BEACH, CHESAPEAKE, SUFFOLK,
HAMPTON, PORTSMOUTH, NEWPORT NEWS, AND ON
THE EASTERN SHORE OF VIRGINIA

757.455.0077

866.455.6657

FAX 757.455.8274

YOUR INJURY, OUR FIGHT!

Essential Information You Should Know Before You Hire
an Attorney or Talk to the Insurance Company

TABLE OF CONTENTS

ACKNOWLEDGEMENTS

JIM HURLEY

I want to thank my family, my lovely wife, Pam and my children, Jimmy and Blair, for putting up with me while I wrote this book. Also, I want to extend my gratitude to David Macaulay, Bill O'Mara, and Griff O'Hanlon for this latest edition. I wish to thank Jim and Kathy Hollomon for their insightful assistance in helping me with this book.

Finally, I would like to thank Ben Glass, Esq., of Great Legal Marketing, LLC, who inspired me to write this book.

JOHN COOPER

My thanks begin with my parents who both practiced law and inspired me to keep up the family tradition of service to others through the legal system. Many mentors and teachers have helped me during my two and half decades, since University of Virginia Law School. My first boss, Judge Becky Smith of the U.S. District Court in Norfolk, Virginia, deserves special credit for motivating me, early on, to strive for excellence in work in the legal profession.

BILL O'MARA

I would like to thank my lovely wife Melissa and our three children for being for my motivation each day. I owe my mentors and colleagues special thanks for all their guidance since entering the practice of law after graduating from Dartmouth College and Washington and Lee University School of Law. Lastly, I would like to thank our clients for giving Cooper Hurley Injury Lawyers the opportunity to fight for you. We appreciate you putting your trust in us.

GRIFFIN M. O'HANLON

My thanks certainly begin with my wife, Kelsey, for always providing steadfast support when the stress of practicing law weighs me down, and my kids for reminding me to never forget to have fun. I also want to extend great thanks to my law partners, Jim, John and Bill, for their dedication, hard-work and encouragement. Cooper Hurley Injury Lawyers would not be able to fully service the needs of our clients without their persistent focus and selflessness.

INTRODUCTION

Cooper Hurley Injury Lawyers is a fast-growing personal injury law firm based in Norfolk, Virginia. Our attorneys have decades of experience in representing people hurt in car accidents and the families of people who have lost their lives in car crashes.

Cooper Hurley Injury Lawyers was created in 2011 when veteran personal injury lawyers John Cooper and Jim Hurley joined forces. The partners already had a long and impressive record of representing car accident clients in the Hampton Roads area and further afield. Attorney Bill O'Mara became a partner in 2017.

The firm grew rapidly to over half-a-dozen attorneys and moved to new offices in downtown Norfolk close to the Circuit Court. It retains its vision of treating clients like family members. Every year, we help hundreds of people who have been hurt in car accidents. Although this is a fast-changing area, the need to protect those who are hurt in accidents from insurance company tricks remains constant. Our personal injury lawyers work on a contingency basis. That means you don't pay us unless we secure a settlement or a trial verdict on your behalf.

As well as our main office in Norfolk, Cooper Hurley Injury Lawyers has client meeting locations in Virginia Beach, Chesapeake, Suffolk, Portsmouth, Newport News, Hampton, and on the Eastern Shore of Virginia. We meet clients at these locations or can come to your home or your hospital bed. We represent people hurt in car wrecks across Virginia and in North Carolina. This book deals with car accident law in Virginia only.

Jim Hurley has represented people hurt in motor vehicle accidents for almost three decades. He limits his practice almost exclusively to helping clients after they were injured in car, truck, and motorcycle accidents.

Jim Hurley became a lawyer to help people. He received his undergraduate degree from the University of Arizona in Tucson, Arizona. He graduated from Thomas M. Cooley Law School in Lansing, Michigan in 1990 and finished 10th in his class of 143. He is a member of the American Association for Justice, American Bar Association, Virginia Trial Lawyers Association, Virginia State Bar Association, and the Norfolk & Portsmouth Bar Association.

Jim Hurley is recognized by Virginia Super Lawyers, a designation attained by less than 5 percent of the Commonwealth's attorneys. He has been awarded an AV Rating by Martindale-Hubbell, the highest rating given, for his practice of law. He is ranked 10 out of 10 "Superb" by Avvo – another attorney rating service.

Jim Hurley has resolved hundreds of cases for his clients but has also litigated numerous cases in Virginia to get clients what they deserve. He has tried and argued cases in federal and state courts and presented cases to the Supreme Court of Virginia. We are always prepared to litigate.

"At Cooper Hurley Injury Lawyers, we believe that we must be prepared to litigate a case to protect our clients' rights. I spend extensive time with my clients to prepare them for trial. As a trial lawyer, it is one of my most important jobs to help my clients understand the litigation process. During my career, I have tried more than 100 jury trials and have been involved in thousands of cases that settled before trial," he said.

Jim Hurley says he uses his extensive experience to get his clients the "best results possible" for their serious injuries.

"At Cooper Hurley Injury Lawyers, our job is to take care of all of our clients' legal needs when they are injured in a car, truck or motorcycle accident. Our clients can focus on getting better from the injuries that they suffered," Jim Hurley said.

John Cooper was born in Norfolk and raised in Virginia Beach. He has worked as a personal injury lawyer for more than three decades. John Cooper received his undergraduate degree at the University of California and his J.D. in law from the University of Virginia.

John Cooper is active in the Hampton Roads community. He is a Governor-at-Large of the Virginia Trial Lawyers Association, a role that involves organizing continuing legal education seminars for lawyers across Virginia. He is an active member of the Virginia Beach Bar Association and the Norfolk & Portsmouth Bar Association.

John Cooper is recognized by Virginia Super Lawyers. He holds an AV Rating by Martindale-Hubbell, the highest rating given, for his practice of law. He is rated 10 out of 10 "Superb" by Avvo and is ranked among the top 100 trial lawyers in Virginia.

John Cooper has worked extensively on cases involving traumatic brain injuries and has extensive experience with wrongful death cases. He secured a $3.5 million settlement for a child whose young father died when the vehicle he was a passenger in was rear-ended by a careless truck driver.

"I have handled injury litigation in every court in Hampton Roads, including Norfolk, Virginia Beach, Portsmouth,

Chesapeake, Hampton, Newport News, and Suffolk. I pride myself on working hard to serve my clients. I hope this book will help you if you or a loved one suffers an injury in an auto accident," John Cooper said

Bill O'Mara attended Dartmouth College and Washington and Lee University Law School. He started his legal career in 2008 when he returned to his home town of Chesapeake. He gained extensive courtroom and trial experience, including contested trials before judges and juries across Hampton Roads. He joined Cooper Hurley Injury Lawyers as an associate attorney in 2014. He became a partner in 2017. He dedicates his entire practice to helping injured people and has represented hundreds of people after they were hurt in car accidents.

Bill O'Mara is an active member of the Virginia Beach Bar Association, the Norfolk & Portsmouth Bar Association, and the American Association for Justice.

He is rated a "rising star" by Virginia Super Lawyers. Just 2.5 percent of young attorneys receive this accolade. Bill O'Mara is rated 10 out of 10 "superb" by Avvo.

THIS BOOK DOES NOT OFFER LEGAL ADVICE

We are happy that you have this book so you can increase your knowledge and understanding of what happens when you are hurt in a car accident in Virginia. However, reading this book does not create any type of attorney-client relationship. The information in this book does not give specific legal advice about your matter. We are not allowed to give any type of legal advice in this book. We are simply offering information to help you. Please note that the information in this book is not legal advice. Our firm cannot represent you until you have agreed to hire us and we have agreed, in writing, to accept your personal injury case. All the information in this book is based on car accidents in Virginia.

CHAPTER 1
CAR ACCIDENTS IN VIRGINIA

Nobody wants to be involved in a car accident. Many of us believe car accidents are unfortunate events that happen to other people. We see crushed cars and emergency vehicles by the roadside, but remain detached. Statistics suggest otherwise. The insurance industry calculates the average driver files a claim for a collision once every 17.9 years. Most of us will be involved in three or four car accidents in our lifetimes.

Although fatal accidents occur every week in Virginia, the odds of being involved in a fatal car crash are low. The National Safety Council points out only three out of every 1,000 car accidents involve a death.

While most of us assume we will never be injured in a car wreck, this is often wishful thinking. Every year, car accidents injure 2 million people in the United States. They cause more than 65,000 injuries on the roads of Virginia annually.

Most of us are woefully unprepared for an accident. Sadly, many accident victims make mistakes in the hours and days after a wreck that stop them recovering the money they deserve and need for their injuries. In this book, we describe car crashes, injuries, insurance company tricks, and how Cooper Hurley Injury Lawyers can help you. Drivers involved in fender benders may not need to hire a lawyer. People who are injured should seek legal advice.

Official figures reveal the roads of America are becoming more dangerous. That's a shocking finding in an era when car manufacturers spend billions of dollars on safer cars and self-driving technology allowing vehicles to sense hazards ahead.

Every year, as many as 40,000 people die on the highways of the United States. About 800 of those deaths are in Virginia. The 65,000 injuries every year on the roads of the Commonwealth equates to the population of a mid-sized city. About 42,000 crashes cause injuries. Double that number cause property damage.

Police in Virginia Beach, the largest city in the Commonwealth, record about 6,500 crashes every year, about 25 deaths and more than 3,000 injuries.

All the improved safety features, the campaigns, and the zero-tolerance enforcement of drunk and distracted drivers is failing to make significant inroads in the problem.

One of the first calls people usually make after a car accident is to their insurance company. Crashes usually cause significant property damage to your vehicle. You want to get back on the road or to obtain a rental car.

Injuries add another dimension to the equation. When a car crash hurts drivers and passengers, it often causes anger as well as pain. You want to talk to the insurance company of the driver who hit you. You want the insurance company to tell you your medical bills are covered.

Unfortunately, car accidents in Virginia are not so straightforward. From the time of the accident, the other side's insurance company will be looking for reasons not to pay for your injuries and property damage or to reduce its payments. The insurance adjusters know you are vulnerable after a car accident and will seek to make you sign away your rights or make mistakes that harm your case.

This book highlights the many tricks insurance companies use to deprive you of money you deserve. It describes the types of car accident in Virginia, the injuries caused by car accidents, and whether you have grounds to file a lawsuit.

It outlines the role that a personal injury lawyer plays in car accident cases. We hope *The Best Book About Virginia Car Accidents and Injuries* will address your questions and concerns and save you from making mistakes. This book does not answer specific concerns realted to your case. We recommend you call Cooper Hurley Injury Lawyers for a free consultation about your Virginia car accident. Call us at (757)-231-6288.

CHAPTER 2

CAR INSURANCE: WHAT YOU NEED TO KNOW

WHAT IS CAR INSURANCE?

Insurance is a contract between you and the insurance company. You pay money, which is called a premium, and the insurance company will cover you for various items when you have a car accident. The insurance policy is long and complicated because of the various laws that govern these policies, but there are several key areas of coverage:

1. **Liability** – This protects the person that causes the car accident, providing a lawyer, and paying for damages caused up to the amount of the policy limits.

2. **Uninsured/Underinsured Motorist Coverage** – This protects you if the person that causes the car accident has no insurance. Also, this coverage protects you if the other driver who caused the crash has less insurance coverage than you have.

3. **Property Damage** – This takes care of the property damage to someone else's car caused by the policyholders. Many people believe that they have "full coverage" with their vehicle insurance policy. There really is no such thing as full coverage in Virginia for car insurance. In fact, because it is legal to drive a motor vehicle in Virginia without motor

vehicle insurance under certain circumstances, often "full" coverage just means enough coverage to protect the bank that loaned you money to buy the car. Unfortunately, most people have no idea what type of insurance coverage they have to protect themselves if they get hurt in a car accident. Many people do not have enough coverage to protect themselves if they were hurt badly in a wreck. It is important to have the adequate amount of insurance coverage to protect yourself and your family. If you are hurt in a car accident, you may have injuries that require expensive medical care. A short stay in a hospital can produce thousands of dollars in medical bills. Besides the medical bills and the pain from the injuries, the inability to work caused by an injury can impact your life. People don't think about these issues when they take out insurance. It is crucial that you carry an insurance policy with the adequate amount of coverage. Many people have only the minimum coverage on their car insurance policy of $25,000 / $50,000. With higher limits, you may help yourself if you are harmed by a driver with inadequate coverage.

(A RECIPROCAL INTERINSURANCE EXCHANGE)

VIRGINIA PERSONAL AUTO POLICY
AMENDED DECLARATIONS
(ATTACH TO PREVIOUS POLICY)
Named Insured and Address

			POLICY NUMBER
Sum 03	Veh		
VA 12 12	Ter		

POLICY PERIOD: (12:01 A.M. standard time)
EFFECTIVE OCT 06 2005 TO JAN 11 2006
OPERATORS

Description of Vehicle(s)

VEH	YEAR	TRADE NAME	MODEL	BODY TYPE	ANNUAL MILEAGE	IDENTIFICATION NUMBER	VEH USE SYM	Miles Per Week
03	99				12000		11 W 06	4

The Vehicle(s) described herein is principally garaged at the above address unless otherwise stated.
VFH 03 VIRGINIA BEACH VA

This policy provides ONLY those coverages where a premium is shown below. The limits shown may be reduced by policy provisions and may not be combined regardless of the number of vehicles for which a premium is listed unless specifically authorized elsewhere in this policy.

COVERAGES ("ACV" MEANS ACTUAL CASH VALUE)	LIMITS OF LIABILITY	VEH 03 6-MONTH D=DED AMOUNT	PREMIUM $	VEH 04 6-MONTH D=DED AMOUNT	PREMIUM $	VEH D=DED AMOUNT	PREMIUM $	VEH D=DED AMOUNT	PREMIUM $
PART A - LIABILITY									
BODILY INJURY EA PER	$ 25,000								
EA ACC	$ 50,000								
PROPERTY DAMAGE EA ACC	$ 25,000								
PART C - UNINSURED MOTORISTS									
BODILY INJURY EA PER	$ 25,000								
EA ACC	$ 50,000								
PROPERTY DAMAGE EA ACC	$ 25,000								
PART D -									
MEDPAY	$ 1,000								

VEHICLE TOTAL PREMIUM

TOTAL PREMIUM - SEE FOLLOWING PAGE(S)

LOSS PAYEE

A 0200000   0200000

Above is a sample of part of a motor vehicle insurance policy, referred to as a "Declaration Page," that summarizes the exact nature and type of coverage under this motor vehicle insurance policy. If you understand what the coverages are in your insurance policy, you are a rare person.

What does this $25,000 / $50,000 mean? This particular coverage on the Declaration Page shown as $25,000 / $50,000 states that the coverage for any one person injured in the accident is $25,000 and the total coverage available for that particular accident is $50,000 when multiple people are injured in the accident. If you have $25,000 / $50,000 coverage, the most an accident victim can recover is $25,000. The $25,000 is all that is available per person. Once the insurance company has paid out the $25,000, there is no more insurance money available for that person on this policy, regardless of the nature of the injuries, the extent of the job loss, or the permanency of the injuries.

In the sample motor vehicle insurance policy, the uninsured motorist coverage is $25,000, which is extremely low, but many people have only $25,000 uninsured motorist coverage. Why is uninsured motorist coverage such an important thing to protect you in case there is a motor vehicle accident? If a drunk driver runs a red light and slams into your car and injures you, your uninsured motorist coverage may be crucial in obtaining any fair results for the accident. If the drunk driver has no car insurance, your uninsured motorist coverage protects you but only to the extent of the coverage you have, which means you have $25,000 uninsured motorist coverage in the particular example. If you had more coverage, then you might get more in this case.

Besides the uninsured insurance coverage, your insurance policy can also protect you through your underinsured coverage. If the person that caused the motor vehicle accident only had a minimum insurance policy of $25,000, your underinsured insurance coverage can protect you to the extent you carried more than the minimum. If you have an insurance policy with more coverage than the at-fault driver, then you may be allowed to recover under this insurance coverage for the injuries you suffered. It's crucial to have adequate car insurance coverage. Most people think that increasing their insurance coverage would cost too much money but usually, the increased coverage does not cost nearly as much money as you think and could help you or your family if hurt in a motor vehicle accident. Simply call your insurance company and ask them about increasing your coverage.

WHAT IS MEDICAL PAYMENTS COVERAGE?

Medical payments coverage is also known as medical benefit coverage or medical expense coverage. This optional coverage on your auto policy allows for payment of some medical bills when you are injured in a motor vehicle accident in your car or anyone else's. Medical payment coverage can reimburse you for medical bills associated with an injury from a car accident, regardless of who is at fault for the accident. You paid for this coverage so use it if you have it. Please note that this medical payment coverage applies even if you have health insurance coverage that also covers your medical bills and, unfortunately, many people do not even know they have this coverage. They never inquire about possible reimbursement of their medical bills. When you use med pay, the defendant's insurer is still responsible for the full amount of the bills as if you did not have the coverage. As shown on our sample automobile insurance policy there is $1,000 for medical payment coverage that can be reimbursed directly to you for medical bills up to $1,000. If you have multiple vehicles on this policy, then the number of vehicles will multiply this medical expense coverage times, the number of vehicles on the policy. So if you have two vehicles on the policy and you have $1,000 of medical payment coverage, you actually have a total of up to $2,000 that you can be reimbursed for your medical bills. Med pay is a really good deal for the consumer and can be bought for very little premium dollars.

HOW DOES PROPERTY DAMAGE COVERAGE WORK?

Initially, the most frustrating thing about a motor vehicle accident is trying to deal with the insurance company about the property damage to your vehicle. Immediately after the accident, you should call your insurance company to report the accident. Also, call the defendant's insurance company to report the property damage to your vehicle. If fault is clear, the defendant's insurance company should accept responsibility and agree to fix your vehicle or give you a check if it is a total loss. You can take your vehicle to a repair shop you choose. While your car is getting fixed, the defendant's insurance company should give you a comparable rental vehicle. If your car is totaled, you get the rental until they give you a check.

Unfortunately, many times the defendant's insurance company will not agree to fix your vehicle immediately because the defendant's insurance company states that it is investigating who is responsible for the accident. Rather than waiting for days on end, you can go ahead and ask to fix your vehicle through your own insurance company. This is often the easy solution if the at-fault insurer is dragging its feet, and if you have the right coverage on your policy to allow this. You will have to pay the deductible. At some point down the road, you may be able to get your deductible back from the defendant's insurance company after they determine the accident was the fault of the other person. If you do not have the necessary comprehensive coverage, then you could have a real problem because your insurer will not pay to fix the car. If you lack rental coverage, you will have no rental car while your car is getting fixed.

The at-fault driver's insurance company only has to repair your vehicle according to the previous condition of your vehicle. The culpable driver's insurance company often authorizes used parts for your repairs as well as fixing only the damaged parts. Although your vehicle will be fixed, it may not be to your complete satisfaction. You can also ask the insurer for money for the decreased value of the car as now wrecked and fixed.

The at-fault driver's insurance company can also declare your car a total loss and simply give you the fair market value which is often less than what you owe on the vehicle, so that you have no vehicle and no money after an accident. If you think that you can have the vehicle fixed, then you have the option of buying the damaged vehicle as scrap from the insurance company for a minimum amount of money.

Property damage often causes many problems, but the most important thing is to stay on top of the situation to either get your vehicle fixed or get as much money for your vehicle as you can. If Cooper Hurley Injury Lawyers is representing you on a personal injury claim, we will also guide you through the property damage.

WHY IS IT IMPORTANT TO UNDERSTAND YOUR INSURANCE COVERAGE?

Knowledge of the insurance policy covering you is crucial and the ability to protect yourself financially after a car accident depends on the amount of insurance coverage that you have. One good reason to hire Cooper Hurley Injury Lawyers is that we know this system well and can help maximize your recovery.

CHAPTER 3
UNINSURED AND UNDERINSURED POLICIES IN VIRGINIA

UM/UIM INSURANCE

FOR HIT-AND RUN OR UNDERINSURED WRECKS

Uninsured and underinsured motorist (UM/UIM) coverage are two types of insurance protection you can take out on your own automobile insurance. It makes sense to pay the premiums for this coverage. If an uninsured or an underinsured driver crashes into you, you may not be able to claim enough to cover your injuries or damage to your car.

These policies are used most frequently in the following scenarios:

1. You were injured by a driver with no insurance or inadequate insurance;

2. You were hurt by a hit-and-run driver who was never identified.

Uninsured motorist coverage is designed to protect you if you've been injured by an at-fault driver who lacks any insurance.

If you have been hurt by someone who does not have their own car insurance, your own car insurance company steps in and provides money for you up to available UIM limits. Underinsured motorist coverage provides additional potential financial insurance recovery above and beyond the liability insurance the at-fault driver has.

If you carried $50,000 in Underinsured Motorist Coverage and you were hit by a driver with a minimal $25,000 coverage, you would have up to $50,000 available to you - $25,000 from the at-fault driver and another $25,000 from your insurance company which would bridge the gap.

The easiest way to know if you have UM or UIM coverage is to look at the declarations page of your insurance policy. You should carry this in your car's glove box but most insurance companies now have apps that allow you to pull up your policy on your smartphone.

Look for the words "uninsured" or "underinsured motorist coverage." Your declarations page should contain two numbers. One relates to liability per-person and the other liability per occurrence.

Anyone who is hurt in the accident can potentially recover up to the maximum of the "per person" number detailed in your insurance policy.

The "per occurrence" figure limits the total payout. If the policy lists a "per occurrence" figure of $75,000 and six people were injured in a car wreck, the most all of the victims combined stand to get is $75,000.

The minimum levels of available UM/UIM insurance in Virginia are:

- $25,000 bodily injury per person;
- $50,000 motorist bodily injury per incident;
- $20,000 per vehicle in property damage.

UIM/UM coverage plays a role in as many as a third of personal injury cases in Virginia. Often, people involved in an accident lose out by not carrying a higher amount of uninsured or underinsured coverage.

UM and UIM policies are important and can be obtained cheaply. Although drivers are required to carry insurance in Virginia, as many as 10 percent of drivers lack insurance, according to the Insurance Research Council. You are only required to have $25,000 of liability car insurance and some states require just $15,000 of liability insurance coverage. If another driver causes serious injuries to you or a family member and only has a $25,000 liability policy, you will likely need to use your UIM coverage to pay for your expenses.

Get as much UM/UIM coverage as you can on your auto accident policy. Paying a small premium can make a big difference if you were hurt in a wreck.

If you are in an accident that's not your fault, you will submit a claim to the other driver's insurance company. However, it's important that you notify your own insurance company about a potential claim. In UM cases, you make a claim with your own insurance company.

WILL MY INSURANCE PAYMENTS GO UP IF I MAKE A UM/UIM CLAIM?

Some people hurt in a car accident are wary of making a claim on uninsured or underinsured motorist coverage because they fear their insurance premiums will rise.

In fact, the insurance companies do not and will not increase your family's automobile insurance rates if you make a claim like UM/UIM or Medpay, all of which are based not on your fault but on somebody else's fault.

The whole purpose of UM and UIM coverage is that your insurance company has already been paid to cover some things which may occur that injure you or your family members or the occupants of your vehicle. If you pay the premiums for these policies, don't be afraid to make a claim after you are hurt in an accident.

CHAPTER 4
CAR INSURANCE COMPANY DIRTY TRICKS

We've heard all the reasons why people sometimes choose not to hire an injury lawyer. They didn't want to make it a big deal. They thought they could handle their case on their own. They wanted to avoid paying an attorney fee from the case. These considerations fail to take insurance company dirty tricks into account.

One of the biggest mistakes car accident victims make is to believe they can trust or outsmart the insurance company. Insurance companies hire very polite people. They adopt a reassuring tone that puts you at ease. They fool you into believing your best interests are their main consideration when it's really saving money for the insurance company.

People may be hesitant about hiring a lawyer. They incorrectly fear they will have to pay a lot of money up front. We've also heard people say they didn't hire a lawyer because it's not about the money, and that they're "not that type of person."

However you decide to handle your injury claim, or whatever your motives, it boils down to being treated fairly. After reading the information below, you'll have serious doubts about whether you'll be treated (or paid) fairly by an insurance company without the help of an experienced personal injury attorney.

We were contacted by a person hit by a car while walking to work. He was kind enough to allow us to use his personal experience with the insurance company to allow you to avoid falling for some common insurance tricks.

After the accident, the at-fault driver's insurance company immediately admitted fault, leaving our client with a false sense that he would be treated fairly. He attempted to handle the case on his own until he reached out to us after receiving these e-mails from the at-fault driver's insurance company:

Good morning, ██████:

This is a follow up of our conversation this morning regarding settlement of your injury claim. I have confirmed that, of the incurred bill of $22,506 at Sentara, $17,717 was written off after payment of $3702 by BCBS and that there was a remaining balance to you of $1086. of the $937 for the radiology bill, $436 was paid and the rest written off. There should be a separate bill for the emergency room doctor and I do not have the bill, but have projected an additional $750 for that, along with the $586 for the ambulance.

we have offered $9,000 for settlement of your injury claim. Please feel free to give me a call at your convenience with any questions or concerns you may have.

Thanks.

██████ | Auto Liability Claims | Virginia-DC Claim Center

Dirty Trick #1: The insurance company will offer to pay only your copays and disregard write-offs.

In Virginia, You are entitled to payment for all reasonable medical bills related to the injury. This means you are entitled to payment for the actual charge made by the hospital or healthcare provider. In the above e-mail, the client had a $22,506 emergency room bill, but the insurance company is offering to pay only $3,702!

The insurance company should have to pay the entire $22,506 bill, and should not attempt to benefit from your own health insurance, which you or your employer pay hard earned money for every month. We are aware of at least one instance in which an insurance company made a lowball offer and had the nerve to ask the injured person to ask his own doctors to lower their bills so it could get off cheaper.

Insistence upon full payment of this single bill alone is 2.5 times larger than the entire settlement offer made by the insurance company. An experienced personal injury lawyer will insist upon full payment of the bill. Most insurance companies don't even attempt this dirty trick on lawyers.

Don't be fooled by the polite tone of e-mails like this. The insurance company's goal is to pay you as little as possible. There's more. After the client asked for clarification, the at-fault driver's insurance company sent another e-mail:

Good morning, ▇▇▇▇. The full amount of $9,000 is coming to you. Whether or not your health insurance carrier comes back to you for reimbursement of what they paid out, I cannot answer. It appears that at six months post accident, they would have notified you. That said, the most they will ask is what they paid out, which is $3702.25 for the ER and $348.82 for the radiology bill. I did not receive the ER doctor's bill but projected $750 for that bill and your insurance would have paid a portion of that.

I hope I have answered your questions to your satisfaction, but if not, please feel free to give me a call.

Thanks.

▇▇▇▇▇▇▇▇ | Auto Liability Claims | Virginia-DC Claim Center

Dirty Trick #2: The insurance company wants to be done with you, and can't be bothered to worry about your future exposure and liabilities.

The insurance company is dangling a $9,000 settlement offer in front of the client by telling him that it is "coming to you," which is technically true in that a $9,000 check will be mailed to him in exchange for a full release- *i.e.*, the case is closed and the insurance company will never pay you more.

The $9,000 may, however, not entirely belong to the client. Some health insurance plans are entitled to be repaid out of personal injury settlements. The insurance company is careful to mention that the client's health insurance company could request payment of $4,801.07 after-the-fact. If the health insurance is owed part of the settlement, then suddenly that $9,000 settlement is more than cut in half, which is apparently of no concern to the at-fault driver's insurance company.

The insurance company is careful to admit that it does not know if the client's health insurance has a right to repayment from the settlement, but shamefully nudges him toward accepting the settlement by suggesting that "they would have notified you" by now since six months have passed since the accident happened.

Insurance Company Dirty Tricks

Being Your Friend

The representative of the car insurance company may be friendly and appear to be on your side. You should be aware the insurance adjuster is not your friend. Even your own insurance company may try to low ball you in the settlement of a claim. Seek the advice of a lawyer who is on your side.

Checking Your Social Media

The Insurance company and its lawyers may check your social media posts after an accident. Don't post details of your five-mile run or any exercise. The insurance company will claim you were not injured. Do not discuss your case on social media. If possible, suspend your account for the duration of the legal case.

This is simply not true, and the suggestion otherwise is dishonest. It is true that some health insurances are not entitled to reimbursement, and sometimes a health insurance plan that is entitled to repayment never seeks it. His health insurance plan, however, through scanning diagnostic codes in your records, or through questionnaires, may contact him long after the accident, and possibly well after the settlement money is spent, and insist upon immediate payment of $4,801.07. If he does not have the money in-hand, the health insurance plan can pursue him for violating the terms of the health insurance plan.

The safest and best practice is to have an experienced personal injury law firm proactively contact your health insurance company to determine if it has reimbursement or subrogation rights. If there are no reimbursement rights, then you will have peace of mind in knowing that you won't get a big bill after-the-fact.

If your health insurance does have reimbursement rights, then it can be handled on the front end, and the amount owed possibly negotiated to allow you to pocket a larger portion of the settlement.

Dirty Trick #3: The insurance company "admitting fault" or "accepting liability" does not mean you'll be paid fairly

Even if the insurance company "admits fault" or "accepts liability" it does not mean you will be paid fairly. It simply means that for the purposes of settlement discussion, the insurance company is not disputing that its driver was at fault.

They will still attempt to negotiate as low of a settlement as you will allow. Also, they can change their mind at any time, and in many instances if the case ends up in court the lawyers for the insurance company will dispute fault.

Dirty Trick #4: *If you happen to be dealing with your own insurance company, it doesn't mean you will be treated more fairly*

Sometimes, coincidently, the at-fault driver happens to have the same insurance company as you. There are also occasions where an uninsured motorist injuries you, so you'll have to negotiate with your own insurance company under your uninsured motorist coverage. Don't be lulled into thinking you will be taken care of simply because you are a loyal customer of the company and always make your payments on time. Your own insurance company will fight you just as hard as anyone else to pay you as little as possible.

Dirty Trick #5: *Not hearing from the insurance company and delay as deadlines approach*

In Virginia, the deadline to file a personal injury lawsuit is typically two years from the date of the accident. Often someone injured in an accident thinks he has plenty of time to attempt to handle the case himself. He thinks if he gets lowballed, then he can always hire a lawyer later. He feels confident because the insurance adjuster seemed sympathetic and caring, and "accepted responsibility."

It is not uncommon for our law firm to receive calls from people 20+ months after the accident panicked that they can't get the insurance company to call them back. Or upset that they waited all this time just to have the insurance company request five years of pre-accident medical records, so it can argue that your problems are from a pre-existing condition.

If you've reached this late state without an attorney, the insurance company has all the leverage. Some lawyers are often hesitant to undertake an injury case very close to the deadline to file a lawsuit, and insurance companies know this. An insurance company can then offer you an unfair settlement. Without a lawyer involved, you are simply not viewed as a legitimate threat to file a lawsuit to insist upon fair payment.

At the end of the case, our client, who was kind enough to share his e-mails with you ended up better off, avoided additional aggravation, and slept easier knowing the case was handled properly. His only regret was not involving Cooper Hurley Injury Lawyers sooner.

These are just a few examples of dirty tricks insurance companies use to avoid paying unrepresented people fairly. These techniques are how they continue to take advantage of people for profit. While every case is different, and not all cases necessarily require the help of an experienced personal injury lawyer, we encourage you to contact us for a free consultation. Don't let the insurance company take advantage of you.

Not Paying Medical Bills

The insurance company should pay all of your medical bills. However, some insurance companies will try to only cover co-pays. Some insurance companies have asked accident victims to request their doctors submit lower bills to save the insurance company money.

Saying You Must Make a Statement

The Insurance company may tell accident victim they must immediately make a statement providing their injuries and damage. The goal is to panic the claimant into self-incrimination Often, these statements are recorded so they can be used late at trial, if necessary, to discredit the injury victim

CHAPTER 5
THE LEADING CAUSES OF CAR ACCIDENTS

Cooper Hurley Injury Lawyers help people harmed in many different accidents. The most common causes of accidents are excess speed, drunk driving, distracted driving, and carelessness. However, many aspects of bad or reckless driving cause serious accidents in Virginia.

Bad driving causes many accidents. Even in poor weather conditions like ice and snow, another driver is usually at fault for the wreck that caused your injuries. You may not always realize another driver was to blame for your accident. An experienced injury lawyer will examine police reports and other details of the accident to get to the cause of what happened. The lawyer will use subpoenas, which are requests for documents, to obtain evidence and cross-examine witnesses during depositions. On occasions, attorneys will use experts to strengthen your case.

Car accidents are seldom straightforward. They may involve numerous parties. The following are some common causes of car crashes in Virginia.

DISTRACTED DRIVING

The rapid development of smartphone technology and social media sites such as Facebook and Instagram in recent years has made distracted driving one of the leading causes of car accidents.

Before smartphones, drivers were distracted by the radio, food and drink, passengers or simply being lost in their thoughts. Technological advances made the issue far worse.

The U.S. Department of Transportation states you take your eyes off the road for about 5 seconds if you send a text while driving. At 55 mph, that's the equivalent of driving the length of an entire football field with your eyes closed. Texting while driving is illegal in Virginia. However, distracted driving is a massive problem in the state. Distracted drving causes about 26,000 crashes every year in Virginia, over three times more wrecks than drunk drivers cause. Accident victims injured by distracted drivers have grounds to sue the at-fault driver.

SPEEDING

Excess speed causes almost 30 percent of all crashes. Many drivers ignore speed limits. In some cases, you can still be speeding if you are driving at or below the speed limit in hazardous road conditions.

The hectic nature of 21st century life means many drivers are in a hurry to get to their destinations whether they are going to work, picking up children or heading on a road trip to see relatives at Thanksgiving or on July 4. At the same time, roads are becoming increasingly congested. Traffic may suddenly slow down or stop unexpectedly. When a driver is speeding, he or she has less time to stop.

The Code of Virginia § **46.2-880** outlines how speed relates to average stopping distances. At 30 mph, it takes a car 109 feet to stop once after factoring in driver reaction time. At 70 mph, the stopping distance becomes 387 feet.

According to the National Highway Traffic Safety Administration, speeding kills over 10,000 people every year nationally, accounting for 27 percent of road deaths. Excess speed causes more than 23,00 crashes a year in Virginia and about 300 deaths. This is 37 percent of all fstsl wrecks in the Commonwealth.

Speeding drivers cause about 13,000 injuries a year on the roads of Virginia, representing about one in five of all injuries.

Drivers who cause crashes while speeding will typically be cited and may be charged with an offense like reckless driving.

DRUNK DRIVING

Drivers who get behind the wheel after drinking alcohol or taking drugs are a major cause of accidents. Drinking alcohol affects vision, tracking, reaction times, coordination and concentration.

Centers for Disease Control and Prevention states about 10,500 people die in alcohol-impaired driving crashes every year. Drunk driving accounted for 28 percent of all traffic-related deaths in the United States. Intoxicated driving is often

Deaths from Drunk Drivers

Virginia has seen a slight decrease in deaths from drunk drivers in recent years but hundreds of people lose their lives to intoxicated drivers every year. In 2017, 248 people were killed in DUI wrecks in the Commonwealth and 4,430 were injured.

Drunk Driving Myths

The following won't sober you up if you get behind the wheel after drinking alcohol...

Black Coffee

Exercise

A cold shower

Cold Air

Eating Food

Drinking Lots of Water

Taking a Quick Nap

Being sick

associated with other high-risk behaviors like being distracted behind the wheel and speeding.

Enforcement campaigns in Virginia helped cut the number of deaths from drunk drivers in Virginia over the last decade. However, drunk drivers claim about 250 lives and injure more than 4,000 people a year in the Commonwealth.

Drivers with a blood-alcohol (BAC) level of 0.08 percent or higher are considered impaired under Virginia law. Often drivers who cause crashes record much higher BAC levels.

If a blood or breath test determines that a driver under 21 has a BAC of 0.02 percent or higher, the driver can be cited for driving under the influence.

Drunk drivers often cause very severe injuries. Cooper Hurley Injury Lawyers have sued hundreds of drunk drivers who caused crashes. In certain cases, the victims of drunk drivers in Virginia can recover 'punitive' damages intended to punish the driver that go over and above the compensation for their injuries.

RED LIGHT RUNNING AND FAILURE TO YIELD

About 45 percent of all car accidents occur at intersections. Often red light runners and drivers who fail to obey stop signs cause wrecks. Red light runners cause about 165,000 accidents a year. They are responsible for 700-800 deaths.

Drivers who ignore red lights are causing more crashes. The Insurance Institute for Highway Safety suggested more communities are turning off red light enforcement cameras, encouraging people to enter an intersection on a red light.

The Hampton Roads cities of Virginia Beach, Norfolk, Chesapeake, and Newport News have red light enforcement cameras at certain intersections. Drivers who run red lights receive civil penalties of $50. Violations caught on camera cannot be used to increase insurance rates or to give DMV points to motorists.

Video evidence can be crucial in car accident cases. A personal injury lawyer can obtain video footage from cameras at an intersection.

In many cases, there is no video footage. Many accidents occur when a driver fails to stop at a stop sign.

Virginia law states drivers who are entering an intersection with a stop sign should "stop at a clearly marked stop line, or, in the absence of a stop line, stop before entering the crosswalk on the near side of the intersection."

Where there is no marked crosswalk, drivers must stop at the "point nearest the intersecting roadway where the driver has a view of approaching traffic on the intersecting roadway."

The driver at the stop sign must yield the right of way to traffic traveling in either direction.

Drivers who approach a "Yield Right-of-Way" sign are not required to stop unless it is required for safety. Virginia code states the driver approaching the sign should slow down to a speed reasonable for existing conditions. He or she should yield the right-of-way to a driver approaching or entering an intersection from another direction, and stop at a clearly marked stop or yield line if "required for safety."

Proving the driver who hit you failed to stop at a stop sign or did not yield the right of way can be a difficult process. Although a police officer may cite the at-fault driver or set out the driver's failure to stop, police reports are not always accurate. A personal injury lawyer will interview witnesses, research all relevant evidence, and challenge a police report on occasions.

RECKLESS DRIVING

Reckless driving in Virginia is a Class I misdemeanor that can land a driver in prison for up to a year. Although many reckless driving offenses involve excess speed, other types of driving can lead to a reckless driving charge.

Driving with faulty brakes, aggressive driving, passing a school bus with its stop sign up, racing, illegally passing, failing to give proper signals and, driving with an overloaded vehicle can result in a reckless driving charge. When a driver travels at more than 20 mph over the speed limit or at over 80 mph regardless of the speed limit, he or she can be charged with reckless driving.

Reckless driving is different from negligent driving in which a motorist often makes a mistake. Reckless drivers disregard the safety of others. Teen drivers are disproportionately more likely to drive in a reckless manner because they are inexperienced, want to impress their friends or to see how fast their cars can go.

Reckless drivers may also be drunk or distracted. They cause untold misery on the roads of Virginia.

TAILGATING

We have all suffered the annoyance of a car or a truck traveling too close behind us. Tailgating is a dangerous practice and a major cause of accidents. If the car in front encounters a problem and has to suddenly slow down or stop, the tailgating vehicle may not be able to stop in time to prevent a collision.

Keeping a safe following distance is one of the most important rules of defensive driving. It is also the most commonly broken rule. Experts say you should keep a minimum of at least two seconds, ideally three, between you and the car in front of you in dry weather.

Use a fixed object like a tree or a bridge. Once the rear bumper of the car ahead of you passes the object you picked, start to count… one-thousand-one, one-thousand two, one-thousand three. If you don't even get to two before your vehicle passes the object you chose, you are traveling too closely.

The following distance should be doubled to at least four seconds in poor weather like rain, ice, fog or snow.

A survey by the National Highway Traffic Safety Administration found about 17 percent of drivers listed tailgating as a major concern. Rear end accidents are the most common type of wreck on the roads of Virginia. They are linked to back and neck injuries like whiplash. A personal injury lawyer will investigate whether the driver who hit you was tailgating.

DROWSY DRIVING

Driver fatigue causes car accidents and injuries in Virginia every day. When you drive sleep-deprived for many hours, the effects can be as serious as drunk driving. While drunk drivers are often aware of their impaired condition, fatigue can strike suddenly and unexpectedly, causing drivers to drift across the highway or to fail to stop when traffic slows down ahead of them.

According to the National Highway Traffic Safety Administration, fatigue results in 1,550 deaths every year in the United States. Drowsiness causes 71,000 injuries and more than 100,000 accidents every year.

The problem is widespread. As many as 1 in 25 adult drivers aged 18 years or older reported having falling asleep while driving in the previous 30 days, noted Centers for Disease Control.

Research by the AAA Foundation for Traffic Safety found drivers ages 16-24 are nearly twice as likely to be involved in a crash caused by fatigue than drivers ages 40-59. Almost 60 percent of drowsy driving accidents involve a driver who drifts across the road or into the lane of another vehicle. As many as 10 percent of all wrecks are caused by sleepy drivers.

The National Safety Council states driving after going more than 20 hours without sleep is similar to driving with a blood-alcohol concentration of 0.08 percent – the legal limit for impaired driving in Virginia.

Drivers who need cold air to concentrate, miss their exits, have difficulty keeping their heads up, frequently yawn or daydream should pull over and take a break.

BAD WEATHER

Bad weather like snow, ice, and heavy rain causes numerous accidents every year. However, drivers who cause accidents cannot get away with blaming the weather. Wrecks in poor weather conditions are usually caused by drivers who failed to properly adapt to the conditions.

Every year, Virginia sees a massive surge in accidents after a winter storm. Drivers are not used to the challenges of snow. They often drive too fast for the conditions or brake too hard, sending their cars into a skid. Drivers fail to look out for the telltale conditions associated with black ice, or don't increase following distances in a rainstorm.

Driving at or just under a speed limit may not be a safe speed in heavy fog or snow.

According to the Federal Highway Administration, bad weather is a factor in as many as one in five accidents. Although most accidents in bad weather are caused by poor driving, bad weather causes injuries and deaths in its own right. Other parties may be held liable for your accident such as a power company that failed to replace weakened poles blown down in high winds or a landowner who did not remove a dangerous tree that was subsequently blown onto a car during a storm. The owners of businesses that fail to deal with ice in their parking lots in a timely manner can be held liable for accidents and injuries.

WRONG-WAY DRIVING

Wrong-way drivers cause some of the most serious crashes we see in Virginia. Typically, these are head-on crashes at high speeds. They cause terrible injuries.

Wrong-way crashes occur more frequently than most people imagine. They usually take place at night and one driver is heading into oncoming traffic. According to the Federal Highway Administration, wrong-way crashes kill 300 to 400 people each year on average, representing about one percent of the total number of traffic-related deaths on the roads of America.

Although this is a small percentage overall, wrong-way driver crashes are typically more severe than other types of crashes.

Studies suggest as many as 70 percent of drivers heading the wrong way are drunk. Older drivers are more likely to drive in the wrong direction. Wrong-way crashes are also caused by fatigue and distracted driving.

UNSAFE LANE CHANGES

Improper and unsafe lane changes are a significant cause of accidents. Often these crashes are caused by the failure of a driver to look in his or her blind spot. Alternatively, an aggressive driver may overtake and cut in front of another driver, causing a crash. Ice and snow can cause cars to drift across lanes as well as drowsy, distracted or drunk driving.

Unsafe lane changes often cause sideswipe accidents. They may also lead to chain-reaction crashes as other drivers take evasive actions.

ROAD RAGE

Road rage is not a specific offense in Virginia. However, aggressive driving can take many forms and result in a reckless driving charge. Research suggests road rage became a more serious issue in recent years. A report from AAA Foundation for Traffic Safety found nearly 9 in 10 drivers fear road rage is a "somewhat" or "very serious" threat to their personal safety.

As many as 8 million drivers have got out of their car to confront another driver or bumped or rammed another car on purpose. Up to 56 percent of crashes are caused by factors that are consistent with road rage, the AAA study found. These contributory factors to crashes include:

- Tailgating
- Illegal passing
- Erratic lane changes.

There are many causes of car accidents in Virginia. Whatever caused your accident, we will look into it in meticulous detail if we take on your case and look at who or what was liable for an injury or a death.

CHAPTER 6
ESTABLISHING FAULT AFTER A VIRGINIA CAR ACCIDENT

ESTABLISHING FAULT AFTER A CAR ACCIDENT

If a driver stops at a red light and a car approaches, fails to stop, and hits him from behind, causing an injury, fault is a fairly straightforward matter.

However, this is not always the case after a car accident. When two cars are involved in a sideswipe accident, for example, both drivers may argue the other moved into each other's lane. A driver who is hurt making a left turn may claim the driver who hit him was traveling too fast or was drunk. That driver may point out he had the right of way.

Showing who is at fault for a Virginia car accident can be complicated, particularly in chain-reaction crashes involving many vehicles. Some accidents occur in busy areas with plenty of witnesses. Others happen on remote rural roads late at night with no independent witnesses.

An experienced Virginia car accident injury lawyer pieces together the evidence from the crash to build a powerful case against the driver who caused the crash. Lawyers have resources at their disposal that are not available to the general public.

Lawyers spend a lot of time gathering evidence from the accident scene. This is vital to the success of a case.

The first step in evaluating fault is to listen to what our client has to say. Often our client will let us know there were witnesses at the accident scene. We aim to interview witnesses as soon as possible. We always look at the police report. The police officer is skilled in interview techniques. Presumably, he or she spoke to all of the parties involved before and after the collision and was at the accident scene shortly after it occurred. Often the officer issued a citation to one or multiple drivers. That can help determine fault.

Receiving a citation is not a bar on filing a lawsuit. On occasions, police officers are mistaken and we can help you fight your citation in traffic court.

However, Virginia has a strict contributory negligence rule that bars you from making a recovery if you are even 1 percent to blame for an accident. The rule may not apply in cases of 'gross negligence' such as when a speeding, drunk driver runs over a pedestrian who unwisely stepped onto a crosswalk without checking for cars.

GATHERING EVIDENCE AFTER A VIRGINIA CAR CRASH

People who are making a claim for their injuries after a car wreck must prove every aspect of their case for damages. The claimant, described as a plaintiff in a legal action, must show:

1. The driver who hit him owed him or her a duty to drive in a careful and reasonable manner;

2. The driver violated his duty of care through his behavior;

3. The negligent or careless driving caused the victim to suffer injuries;

4. The victim suffered real injuries and losses that require compensation;

It's not easy to prove all of these elements but an attorney must. Evidence gathered by a lawyer may include:

- The police report of the accident;
- Evidence from police body cameras, 911 calls, and police dash cam evidence;
- Admissions in the heat of the moment;
- The observations of eyewitnesses to the crash;
- Any statements or admissions of fault made by the driver who caused the wreck;
- Criminal charges, citations, and traffic court proceedings relating to the case;
- Photographic evidence of the wreck scene by you, other parties or the police officer;
- Safety reports of vehicle roadworthiness;
- Breath and blood test results obtained from DUI suspects;
- Evidence of drug use by the at-fault driver;
- Cellphone records relating to whether the driver was distracted;
- Video evidence from traffic cameras or red light signals;
- Evidence from liability experts. In drunk driving cases, a lawyer will often retain an expert toxicologist;
- Black box data showing the vehicle's speed in the minutes and seconds before an accident. An expert could assist in providing evidence that was correctly downloaded. Although

most new cars now have black boxes, this evidence is more likely to be used in big cases like truck wrecks. Expert accident reconstruction evidence cannot be used in Virginia car accident cases.

THE IMPORTANCE OF CONTACTING YOUR INSURANCE COMPANY AFTER A CAR ACCIDENT

No matter who is at fault in an accident, you should report the incident to your auto insurance company as soon as possible.

Most policies require you to do this. Your insurance company could deny coverage if another party later claims the accident was your fault. Typically, the other party's insurance company will contact you within a few days of a crash. This is often before you have thought of contacting a car accident lawyer. Insurance companies often seek to resolve the property damage claim with you as soon as possible. The insurance claims representative may try to convince you an attorney is not necessary for your personal injury claim. Be aware the insurance company is not on your side. Many people who are involved in a car accident don't feel symptoms in the hours or days afterwards. Accident victims often have undiagnosed conditions like brain injuries. If you rush to settle with the insurance company early on, you may not be able to recover for injuries you discover later.

CHAPTER 7
TYPES OF CAR ACCIDENTS

At Cooper Hurley Injury Lawyers, we help people hurt in a wide range of accidents. Some types of wrecks like rear-enders are very common. Others like rollover crashes and head-on collisions are less common but injuries are typically more severe.

Some car accidents are straightforward. When a driver runs a red light and sideswipes another, liability is clear. However, in a chain reaction accident involving multiple vehicles, many drivers may have made mistakes. It takes a thorough examination by a personal injury lawyer to piece together what happened.

Here are some common types of car accident in Virginia.

REAR-END ACCIDENTS

Rear-end crashes are the most common types of car wrecks. A rear-end collision happens when a driver hits another vehicle from behind in the same lane of travel. Rear-end crashes are associated with neck injuries like whiplash. It's usually obvious which party is at fault – the one who crashed into the back of another car.

However, there are some situations in which the driver who was hit may be to blame. These can include when a car suddenly stops on a fast-moving highway with no good reason or pulls out in front of another.

Although it's usually obvious which driver caused a rear-end accident, you should still consider hiring an attorney. Often rear-end accidents cause serious neck and back injuries. The insurance company may fail to compensate you for what your injuries are worth.

The insurance companies work on a sliding scale relating to payouts. Insurance adjustors use 'plug and play' computer programs to calculate your pain and suffering after a car crash in Virginia. They created these programs to save the company as much money as possible.

SIDESWIPE ACCIDENTS

Sideswipe accidents typically occur when vehicles traveling on a parallel course hit each other. These wrecks are often caused by an improper lane change but determining fault may be tricky. Each party often blames the other. They may also be single-vehicle accidents because a car can sideswipe a crash barrier, a light pole, or a road sign.

There are many reasons for sideswipe accidents. Drivers may fail to notice other vehicles in their blind spots when changing lanes. Distracted, speeding, and drunk drivers also cause sideswipe crashes.

Although sideswipe accidents may not be as serious as T-bone or head-on crashes, they can be fatal if they cause a vehicle to swerve and hit other road traffic or to roll over, or leave the highway and hit trees.

Sideswipe accidents can be particularly serious when a larger vehicle hits a much smaller one such as when a bus or SUV hits a cyclist or a truck strikes a glancing blow to a motorcyclist throwing the rider off their bike.

Often in sideswipe accidents, the initial contact is a prelude to a more serious automobile accident. A driver who hits another car or an inanimate object may overreact by overcorrecting or swerving quickly into the road as a reaction to the initial impact. It may cause a serious rollover or head-on accident or other types of contact with vehicles on the highway.

The Virginia Driver's Manual published by the Department of Motor Vehicles states drivers must check their side and rearview mirrors for traffic approaching from behind them before changing lanes.

Use your turn signal to tell other drivers you plan to change lanes. A study by the Society of Automotive Engineers found failing to use turn signals causes about 2 million crashes a year. First check for other drivers moving into the lane you want to switch to. Shortly before you start moving into the other lane, glance over your shoulder and look out for any vehicles that may be in your blind spot. The manual states that drivers who are changing lanes, passing other vehicles, or entering or leaving a highway must always use their turn signals and check traffic to the rear and sides. When driving on a multi-lane highway, travel in the right lane if you are driving slower than the traffic around you. The left lane is for passing only.

T-BONE ACCIDENTS

Every year, T-bone accidents, also known as broadside accidents or side-impact collisions, claim the lives of up to 10,000 people in the United States.

A T-bone accident occurs when the front of a car, pick-up, van or truck crashes into the side of another vehicle. T-bone accidents usually occur at intersections when a driver fails to stop at a stop sign or traffic signal, or fails to yield the right-of-way to the other driver. T-bone collisions often cause serious injuries. No matter how much side impact protection a car contains, there is only a thin layer of metal between the vehicle that causes the accident and the victim.

T-bone accidents often cause fractures to the legs and arms, spinal fractures and brain injuries.

Side impact collisions frequently involve multiple vehicles. Intersections are busy places. When a car is hit suddenly by another vehicle, it may veer into the path of other vehicles. The broadsided vehicle is often pushed violently sideways toward oncoming traffic. The force of a broadside crash will often spin the striking vehicle. The driver and passenger face secondary collisions and additional injuries.

EJECTION ACCIDENTS

Crashes in which a driver or a passenger is ejected from a car cause extremely serious injuries. People ejected from cars are critically injured or killed at a rate more than three times higher than wreck victims who are not ejected.

Ejection usually involves a driver or a passengers crashing through a sheet of glass at high speed. It exerts tremendous trauma on your body. The accident victim often crashes onto the hard road and may suffer serious head injuries. People who are ejected onto roads are frequently hit by other vehicles.

The National Highway Traffic Safety Administration (NHTSA) states 30 percent of all deaths suffered in car crashes involve an ejection of car occupants. Most ejection victims failed to wear a seatbelt.

There are two forms of ejection – complete and partial. Complete ejection is the most serious kind. The trauma of crashing through glass is compounded by hitting the road.

Occupants who are partially ejected shatter the windshield, or are partially thrown out of a side window but don't end up outside the vehicle. A seatbelt malfunction can cause this kind of ejection. Partial ejections often cause serious injuries.

Wearing a seatbelt is the best way to safeguard yourself against an ejection accident. However, people who fail to wear safety belts are not barred from filing a lawsuit against the driver who hit them. Your case is no different from someone who was wearing a safety belt. Not wearing a safety belt is not a defense the insurance company or its lawyers can use against you.

ROLLOVER ACCIDENTS

Rollover accidents are the most deadly kinds of crash in Virginia or elsewhere. Of more than 9 million car crashes in a given year in the United States, only 2.1 percent involve a rollover. However, these wrecks cause more than 30 percent of all deaths from passenger vehicle crashes. Every year, about 7,500 people lose their lives in rollover crashes.

There is a strong link between deaths and not wearing seatbelts. Almost 70 percent of people who lose their lives in rollover crashes are not wearing a seatbelt. When an accident involves an ejection, the dangers of death or serious injuries are considerably higher.

About 85 percent of rollover accidents are single vehicle wrecks. High-sided vehicles like vans, pickups, and SUVs are more likely to flip in accidents.

The NHTSA found the increasing popularity of SUVs and light trucks is leading to a spike in rollover deaths. High-sided vehicles like SUVs are more prone to flipping over. Although SUV manufacturers are making them safer, you should be wary of driving fast around curves or in high winds. Although most rollover wrecks are single vehicle accidents that are not caused by another vehicle, injured passengers often have grounds to sue a driver.

HEAD-ON COLLISIONS

Head-on collisions occur when the front sections of two vehicles strike each other. They may be a direct hit or at an angle. These are often devastating crashes. The combined force of both of the vehicles causes a horrific impact.

Two cars should not come into contact in this way. Sadly, head-on collisions are common in Virginia. In Hampton Roads, we often see head-on collisions in rural areas like Suffolk where one driver loses control and crosses a center line. More head-on collisions occur on country roads.

Another scenario leading to a head-on crash is when a driver travels the wrong way on a highway or an Interstate. Often these drivers are drunk, distracted or get confused in the dark.

In wrong way crashes, it's clear who is to blame. However, a driver who crossed a line may try to claim you also veered across the road. It's important to hire an experienced car crash injury lawyer when liability is disputed. Even when it's clear who is to blame for a head-on collision, your injuries may be serious enough to require the help of a lawyer.

ROADSIDE ACCIDENTS

Motorists who break down or have to stop by the road due to another emergency are particularly vulnerable to injury. Some of the worst tragedies seen in Hampton Roads in recent years involved broken down cars. People inside disabled cars were hit and killed or they were struck while standing outside their car.

Motorists who break down need to act fast to avoid causing danger to themselves or others. When you break down at the roadside:

- Put your hazards on immediately;
- If possible, get your car to a safe place;
- Call the emergency services;
- If you are in a safe place, remain in your vehicle;
- Never cross the highway;
- Use warning triangles and flares if possible;
- Don't allow children to wander around at the side of the road.

CHAIN-REACTION ACCIDENTS

Chain reaction accidents involve multiple vehicles. They often leave many people dead or injured. America's interstates have witnessed some terrible chain-reaction accidents in ice, fog, or snow involving as many as 80 vehicles. Most chain reaction accidents involve two or three cars. A mistake or reckless driving by one motorist often causes another to swerve and hit a third car. That car may strike another vehicle. Working out who is to blame for a chain-reaction accident is a complicated business. Sometimes more than one driver is to blame. Police have reported some accidents in Hampton Roads in which more than one driver was intoxicated. The complicated insurance issues after a chain reaction accident often make it necessary to hire a personal injury lawyer.

Whatever kind of accident you are involved in, you should seek legal help after an injury. Car accidents are often incredibly stressful and life-altering. Talk to a personal injury lawyer about your options.

TYPES OF CAR ACCIDENTS

MULTI VEHICLE

Multi-vehicle accidents are also known as chain-reaction crashes. They may be complicated and leave numerous people injured.

REAR ENDERS

Rear-enders are the most common type of wreck. The driver who hits a car in front is usually to blame. Neck injuries and whiplash are common.

HEAD ON

Head-on collisions are often deadly. They are typically caused by a driver crossing a center line or a wrong way driver. These accidents combine the forces of two cars.

T-BONE

Drivers and passengers often suffer serious injuries in T-bone accidents because cars have less side protection. T-bone accidents usually occur at intersections when a driver is making a turn.

ROLLOVER

Rollover accidents account for just 2 percent of wrecks but 30 percent of deaths. They are often single vehicle accidents. Failure to wear a seat belt heightens the risk of death or serious injury.

SIDESWIPE

Sideswipe accidents are linked to reckless lane changes and a failure to signal. Although these wrecks can be property damage only, they can cause serious chain-reaction crashes

CHAPTER 8

PUTTING A VALUE ON CAR ACCIDENT INJURIES IN VIRGINIA

We are often asked by clients 'how much is my case worth?' It's not a simple question to answer. Although some damages can be worked out by tried and tested formulas, others are not so easily quantified. There is no such thing as a personal injury calculator in Virginia.

There are two main elements of a personal injury claim -- economic damages and pain and suffering damages. A personal injury claim involves adding up past medical bills, future medical bills, lost wages, and wages likely to be lost in the future. A pain and suffering element is added to the equation. The amount awarded for pain and suffering may exceed the amount given from the other losses. Virginia courts may also add punitive damages in some cases such as the worst instances of drunk driving. This is additional money intended to punish the at-fault driver.

Although attorneys use a formula for assessing past and future medical bills and past and future lost wages, pain and suffering damages typically make up the largest chunk of a personal injury payout. Insurance companies have programs that give pain and suffering a figure. However, there is no guarantee a jury will abide by these formulas if a case makes it to a trial.

TWO KEY ELEMENTS IN CALCULATING PERSONAL INJURY DAMAGES IN VIRGINIA

When you talk to a lawyer about your personal injury case, he or she won't be able to give you an exact figure for what your case is worth. However, two key elements indicate the approximate value of a case. They are:

1. **The extent of injuries**

   An accident victim who suffers a permanent brain injury due to the fault of another driver will be entitled to more money than a claimant who suffers a whiplash injury that lasts a week. Both past and further medical bills, lost wages, and pain and suffering are higher in the first case and the victim may have high ongoing care needs.

2. **Available insurance coverage**

   If you are hit by a driver carrying minimum insurance coverage, you may end up with little money to pay your medical bills. However, multiple insurance policies are available in some cases. At Cooper Hurley Injury Lawyers, we seek to maximize as many policies as possible.

FACTORS USED IN VIRGINIA PERSONAL INJURY CALCULATIONS

Half a dozen key elements are added together to work out a damages claim in personal injury cases. They are:

1. **Lost earnings**

   An attorney can easily calculate the sum of lost income related to your accident. If you used benefits like time-off entitlement because you were injured, a dollar sum will be factored in.

2. **Future lost income**

A projected calculation of how much money you stand to lose in the future due to injuries from an accident is added to the equation. Future lost income is more relevant after a serious injury.

3. **Medical Expenses**

Medical bills are totaled up after an injury. Avoid trying to settle with an insurance company while you are still being treated for an injury. You face losing money.

4. **Future medical expenses**

If you are likely to have recurring medical issues from your injury that require treatment, your Virginia injury lawyer will factor in the likely cost of future medical expenses.

5. **Property Damage**

Property damage may be factored in after a car, truck or motorcycle accident. After an auto accident, you are entitled to be 'made whole' for any damage to your personal property.

6. **Pain and Suffering and a Multiplier**

In calculating pain and suffering, insurance companies often work with multipliers of up to five times your medical costs. After serious injuries, the multiplier may be even higher.

Many of the large insurance companies use an automated formula to calculate pain and suffering. The Colossus computer program, for example, is used by companies including Allstate to estimate total injury claims. These are plug in systems which pay little regard for the claimant's personal circumstances.

rrograms like Colossus are intended to drive down payouts and protect the insurance company's bottom line. Insurance companies often multiply the total of medical bills by a number between one-and-a-half and five to calculate pain and suffering.

Of course, a computer program is not equal to the task of accurately measuring pain and suffering. Programs like this fail to take into consideration factors like emotional trauma from a car accident.

FACTORS TO CONSIDER IN A VIRGINIA INJURY CASE

Unlike the insurance company, a Virginia personal injury lawyer will carefully asses your needs and consider the human factor before working on a reasonable offer in negotiations with the insurance company or taking the case to court. Pertinent factors include:

- The nature of your injuries;
- The duration of pain and suffering;
- How permanent the injury is likely to be;
- How this ordeal impacted your quality of life.
- How much emotional pain and suffering the accident caused.

WHEN IS A HIGHER MULTIPLIER NEEDED IN VIRGINIA PERSONAL INJURY CASES?

In its pain and suffering calculation, the insurance company will likely use a multiplier one-and-a-half to five times your medical costs.

Certain factors may justify a higher multiplier. They include:

- Severe pain associated with your injuries;
- Injuries that cannot ever be successfully remedied;
- A prolonged recovery time and ongoing pain;
- Suffering permanent consequences like disability, scars, disfigurement, psychological issues or concentration and memory problems associated with a brain injury.
- Doctors warning your condition is likely to worsen in the future due to the accident.

THE "PER DIEM" METHOD OF CALCULATING PAIN AND SUFFERING

There is a second method of calculating pain and suffering. It's known as the "per diem" method which means "per day" in Latin. The injured party from a Virginia auto accident or a slip and fall receives a specified dollar amount for every day they live with pain related to the accident under this method.

The "per diem" method is not particularly useful for calculating long-term injuries. One issue is justifying the daily rate used in calculations. A way to calculate the daily rate as being "reasonable" is to use actual, daily earnings. The daily pain caused by injuries is equated to the effort of going to work each day.

THE DANGERS OF FIGHTING THE INSURANCE COMPANY ALONE

Personal injury calculations are notoriously complex. Although the insurance company may tell you it's the case, there is no simple method of assessing overall damages after an accident. You may leave money on the table if you try to fight the insurance company alone. Every case is unique. You should discuss your circumstances with a legal professional.

CHAPTER 9

ACCIDENTS CAUSED BY DEFECTIVE CARS

Bad drivers cause most car accidents. However, in some cases, a vehicle defect can cause a wreck. These cases are different from the typical car accident claim. A product liability claim can be brought against a carmaker or the manufacturer of a part that failed rather than a claim against a driver's insurer.

This is a complicated area of the law. The mere fact a tire blew out or brakes failed on a car causing an accident does not necessary mean the automaker was to blame. Often, the car owner failed to maintain his vehicle properly and is liable for an accident. A workshop may also be sued for shoddy repairs that caused` a crash.

Lawsuits relating to defects on cars can be brought in the following circumstances:

1. A car or a part is of an inherently dangerous design;
2. Poor manufacturing meant the design did not comply with safety standards.

The car industry announced a series of massive recalls due to dangerous defects in recent years. They included:

THE FORD-FIRESTONE TIRE SCANDAL

Separating tires on the Ford Explorer SUV killed more than 200 people in the late 1990s. Bridgestone/Firestone recalled about 6.5 million tires, mostly on the Ford Explorer, at the time, the world's top-selling sport utility vehicle (SUV).

FAULTY GM IGNITION SWITCHES

A defective ignition switch on some smaller General Motors models of cars caused at least 120 deaths and about 300 injuries. The ignition switches failed causing the cars to stall. An independent fund set up to compensate the victims of accidents involving the ignition switches awarded $594.5 million and approved 399 injury and death claims in 2015.

TOYOTA UNINTENDED ACCELERATION

Toyota recalled millions of vehicles from 2009 to 2011 over a mysterious sudden acceleration issue. Drivers claimed their acceleration pedals stuck. An additional issue over an incompatible floor mat was reported. Highway patrol officer and three members of his family were killed after the accelerator in his Lexus became stuck on an incompatible floor mat. The defects were linked to about 90 deaths and many more injuries.

CHRYSLER GAS TANK FIRES

Chrysler recalled 1.5 million Jeep SUVs over vulnerable exposed plastic gas tanks. In a number of instances, the tanks caught fire after the cars were hit from behind. The defect caused at least 50 deaths.

TAKATA AIRBAG RECALLS

Takata is a Japanese manufacturer of airbags. A dangerous defect in the airbags found in millions of different cars led to the largest recall in the history of the car industry and multiple injuries and deaths.

The National Highway Traffic Safety Administration (NHTSA) found an issue with millions of airbags that use an ammonium nitrate-based propellant without a chemical drying agent. The airbags were unexpectedly activating, often during minor fender benders. In some cases, they were exploding, sending shrapnel into drivers or passengers. The problem was associated with humid conditions in the southern states.

More than 37 million vehicles have been recalled in the U.S., involving 49.5 million defective airbags. The defect caused over 20 deaths and multiple injuries.

THE MOST COMMON CAR DEFECTS IN VIRGINIA

Although scandals like GM's faulty ignition switches and Takata's exploding airbags made headlines, the car industry makes recalls every week.

Car manufacturers and makers of parts must follow minimum safety standards. Smart computer technology and research has ensured cars are much safer than three decades ago and motorists are better protected in crashes.

However, issues such as faulty brakes, tire tread separation or blowout, and steering failures cause thousands of deaths every year.

The NHTSA cites tire or wheel failures as the most common factor in accidents caused by equipment failure. It's important to pay close attention to these parts and to get your vehicle serviced regularly. Always comply with recall notices. Your vehicle will be fixed free of charge.

Some motorists are not aware their car is subject to a recall. You can check by looking up your car by vehicle identification number (VIN) on the government's Safercar.gov website.

MAKING PERSONAL INJURY CLAIMS IN THE ERA OF THE SELF-DRIVING CAR

Self-driving cars are hailed as the future of motoring. However, a series of high profile crashes has called the technology into question.

Self-driving cars are meant to make the highways safer by removing the element of driver error. Many newer cars are already fitted with collision-avoidance systems. Sensors on the car slow it down automatically when it gets too close to another vehicle.

Autonomous and semi-autonomous cars are being tested in California, Arizona, and other states. They have been linked to a series of crashes, some of them fatal. Some of accidents involved Tesla's Autopilot, a system that allows the car to accelerate, brake and steer by itself, but is not designed to completely replace a driver.

In another case, an Uber autonomous vehicle hit and killed a pedestrian in Arizona when it failed to stop.

If self-driving cars become commonplace on the roads of Virginia, we can expect to see a radical change in how lawsuits are brought with claims switching from at-fault drivers to manufacturers. However, there are many gray areas and likely questions about the extent of human liability for accidents involving autonomous cars.

If you believe a defect on your car caused your injury, you should talk to an attorney rather than taking on a manufacturer, or another party alone. At Cooper Hurley Injury Lawyers, we have a products liability team who will work with you and sue a manufacturer on your behalf.

CHAPTER 10
TYPES OF INJURIES IN A VIRGINIA CAR ACCIDENT

Injuries in a Virginia car wreck range from common complaints like sprains and soft tissue injuries to severe and life-threatening conditions like quadriplegia and traumatic brain injuries. Although permanent injuries are thankfully rare, the effects of many car accident injuries can linger for months or even years after a crash. Watch out for the signs of injuries after a car wreck. If you have concerns, see your medical provider and seek help from a specialist. Some conditions like brain injuries are notoriously tricky to diagnose and your doctor may fail to pick up on the symptoms initially.

Some types of injuries associated with a car accident include:

WHIPLASH

Whiplash is a non-medical term used to describe cervical acceleration-deceleration (CAD) injuries. When you are hit from behind suddenly, your head is jerked backward and forward suddenly. The abrupt force of the impact stretches and tears the muscles and tendons in your neck.

People who suffer whiplash often report severe pain, tiredness, and blurred vision. Neck pain typically lasts between a few hours and several months after a crash, depending on the severity of the injury. Although most whiplash injuries clear up, some linger. Insurance companies downplay the seriousness of this injury and may offer you less than it's worth.

HERNIATED DISCS

Back injuries are some of the most common complications associated with car accidents. Herniated discs are also known as ruptured or slipped discs. These injuries occur when the impact of an automobile crash causes the soft center of a spinal disc to protrude through a crack in the tougher exterior casing. The spinal discs support the vertebrae. There are 23 of them. Six are cervical discs in the neck. There are 12 discs in the middle back (thoracic region), and five in the lower back (lumbar region).

Attorneys often compare discs to jellied doughnuts that can rupture. When the "jelly" leaks out the core of the disc may intrude into the spinal canal and hit a nerve root. A serious impact during a car accident can cause this extremely painful injury in the upper back or the neck.

A herniated disc may put considerable pressure on the nerve around it, which can cause pain to radiate throughout the person's body. Invasive surgery may be necessary in some cases. You can suffer the effects of a herniated disc for years after a crash. However, some patients recover in about three months.

BROKEN BONES

Car crashes exert enormous force on the human body. Broken bones are a painful and potentially life-altering consequence of a car wreck in Virginia.

Some of the most common fractures include wrist fractures after drivers and passengers put their hands forward during the impact and broken collarbones (clavicles).

Car crashes can also cause broken ribs and vertebrae in the back. Fractures of the skull, the pelvis or the femur (the thighbone) can be life-threatening.

If you break a bone during a car crash, you are likely to require surgery or a cast to heal. People who suffer fractures usually take time off work. They require pain medications, physical therapy, and other costly treatments to heal. In some cases, the bones fail to heal properly and you may face a lifetime of impairment.

It's important to recover enough money to cover the ongoing costs of broken bones.

There are many different types of fracture. You should be aware of the differences and the possible complications. They include:

Transverse – The bone is broken into two pieces from a direct hit in a car crash. The break is usually at a right angle to the long plane of the bone.

Comminuted fracture. In this type of break, the bone shatters into three or more pieces due to a strong impact. Comminuted fractures entail a long recovery time and complications often linger.

Compound – Compound fractures are also very serious. The broken bone often protrudes directly through the skin. Compound fractures entail a higher risk of infection because the skin is broken.

Buckle – A buckle fracture entails a bend or a rupture of the bone but no actual break. Children whose bones are still developing are more likely to suffer from buckle fractures.

Stress – Stress fractures are partial breaks like buckle fractures. They are also more common in children. However, one only one side of the bone fractures and the other side bends.

Oblique – Oblique fractures typically occur in situations where the bone breaks along the diagonal of the long axis. This kind of fracture is relatively rare but can happen in car wrecks if one bone becomes trapped and another bone is twisted over the top of the trapped bone.

Avulsion – When you suffer from an avulsion fracture, the bone separates from the ligaments and tendons. Avulsion fractures often cause acute pain. Surgery is usually required.

Hairline – Hairline fractures are small cracks to the bone. If a car crash leaves you with a hairline fracture, you may not realize at first and fail to get the medical help you require. However, the crack can spread, weakening the bone.

HEAD INJURIES

Head injuries and traumatic brain injuries can cause severe complications. They can lead to long periods off work or you may no longer be able to continue in your job. They can impact sleep, your moods, and your relationships with your family members. However, doctors often fail to diagnose brain injuries in the days and weeks after a car crash unless they are severe. There are many different types of brain injuries including:

Concussions – Also referred to as mild traumatic brain injuries, concussions are the most common types of head injuries suffered in a crash. If you lost consciousness for a short time during a crash you likely suffered a concussion.

Contusion. A contusion injury involves a bruise. A bruise to the brain is a lot more serious than a bruise to the leg or arm and may require surgery to remove.

Diffuse Axonal injury. This type of brain injury is caused by the brain rotating violently. Structures in the brain may tear. Concussions are a mild type of diffuse axonal injury.

Penetration injuries – In some accidents, an object can penetrate the brain. These are very serious injuries and a significant cause of deaths, particularly in young people.

Coup-Contrecoup injuries. These injuries occur at the site of trauma and the opposite side of the brain. The "coup" injury occurs at the initial site of impact. The movement of the brain in the skull causes the second impact against the back of the skull.

ROTATOR CUFF INJURIES

The rotator cuff is a set of muscles and tendons around the shoulder joint. These muscles keep the head of your upper arm bone in the shallow socket of the shoulder. A rotator cuff injury often happens in a car crash. It leads to a dull ache in the shoulder. Sleeping on the side of the injury can exacerbate it. Severe rotator cuff tears often require surgical repair or even joint replacement.

CHEST INJURIES

Chest injuries are common in car accidents. Cars give drivers very little freedom of movement and the chest is vulnerable to collisions with the steering wheel. Even a low impact crash can cause contusions or bruises. More severe car accidents can cause broken ribs or internal injuries.

The chest area may also experience a high degree of force in impacts with seat belt, which can cause severe bruising. Skeletal injuries such as clavicle, rib, and sternum injuries are among the most common car accident injuries. Car accidents cause about 90 percent of all sternum fractures. These injuries can cause complications due to their closeness to the heart and lungs.

BURN INJURIES

Extreme car wrecks can cause fires. When occupants of a vehicle fail to get out in time, fires often prove deadly. Burn injuries can also cause a lifetime of pain and suffering and require multiple surgeries such as skin grafts.

AMPUTATIONS

Car accidents can trap drivers and passengers and cause the loss of a limb like an arm, a leg or a finger. Amputations are more common after motorcycle accidents than car accidents. A disfiguring injury of this nature affects a victim for the rest of their life.

An amputation can be life-threatening. A car crash victim can suffer extreme blood loss. According to the National Limb Loss Information Center, about 1 in 200 people in the United States has suffered an amputation.

KNEE INJURIES

Knees are vulnerable in car crashes. Injuries range from bruises to numerous fractures. Cartilage in the knee may tear if your knee is twisted or turned abruptly in a crash.

SPINAL CORD INJURIES

Spinal injuries can be life-threatening. Even if a victim survives, he or she may need 24/7 care. These injuries attract big settlements and verdicts due to the high cost of ongoing care. There are two main forms of paralysis.

Both **quadriplegia** and **paraplegia** are life-changing results of spinal cord injuries. These conditions will have a profound impact on your day-to-day life, requiring long-term medical assistance. The type of disability resulting from your accident will depend on the area of your spine that was injured. While both quadriplegia and paraplegia can have catastrophic effects on your life and livelihood, there are distinct differences between the two.

PARAPLEGIA

Paraplegia is a condition in which the lower extremities – as well as part of the trunk – become immobilized due to a spinal cord injury. There are two types of paraplegia:

Incomplete paraplegia – You may still be able to sit, balance, and walk.

Complete paraplegia – You will not be able to use your legs and torso at all.

Both types of paraplegia may result in additional problems, such as a loss of bladder control and sexual function.

QUADRIPLEGIA (TETRAPLEGIA)

Patients with quadriplegia experience a loss of sensory and motor functions in all four limbs. In addition to a complete loss of movement, quadriplegia will result in a loss of bladder and sexual function and may result in difficulties breathing. This condition can also produce a burning or tingling sensation throughout the entire body, while interfering with feeling.

People who are involved in car accidents can suffer many types of injuries. This chapter is not a definitive guide to injuries. If you believe a car wreck caused your injury, please call a Virginia accident lawyer.

CHAPTER 11
WHAT TO DO IMMEDIATELY AFTER A CAR ACCIDENT

After a car accident, you need to do the following:

1. Immediately stop your vehicle so that you can take care of the necessary issues. Never leave the scene of an accident as that can result in criminal charges. Call the police. The police will investigate, collect any important information and call ambulances for any injuries. Please remember that the police officer will ask you what happened, and any statement you give the police offer will be written down. Be truthful but careful with what you say and never express opinions that could ultimately hurt you about how the accident happened such as, "I think the accident was my fault."

2. After months go by, most people forget how the car accident happened. It is very important to keep your own journal to record how the accident happened, while it is fresh in your mind. You can use this information at a later date to protect yourself and your family. Also, record how the accident and your injuries affected you emotionally. The following information should be gathered: witnesses' names and addresses, a rough diagram of the crash area, and pictures, including any physical evidence like possible skid marks.

Take video at the scene with your cellphone. Interview witnesses if possible.

3. If you are injured or anyone in your family is injured, it is crucial to get medical treatment. The most important thing in any car accident is to take care of the injuries to you and your family.

4. Other things to note about the accident are road conditions, traffic conditions, weather conditions, the speed of your car before the accident, the speed of the other car before the accident, and the angles of the collision impact.

5. You should be aware many people initially feel no injuries after a car accident. They may believe their injuries are minimal and decline the help of paramedics at the scene of the accident. However, the police officer will always note any injuries, regardless of whether someone seeks treatment. If you tell the officer "I have no injuries. I am fine," this information will be written down. People who later develop injuries face an uphill battle to prove they were hurt in the car crash. The insurance company will use your statement of "no injury" against you in any claim you bring. It is best to tell the police that you think you might be hurt but will drive yourself to the hospital, if you are unsure of the extent of your injury, or just do not want to get in an ambulance.

6. Photographs and video of the area and the damage to any of the vehicles can be helpful at a later date. If you do not get these photographs immediately they may be difficult to obtain later on. The scene may change. For example, debris may be moved by traffic.

7. Finally, you must prepare yourself for the inconvenience, problems, and headaches associated with a car crash and its aftermath.

8. The other driver's insurance company adjuster may call you right after the accident to try to get you to give a recorded statement or take a quick, low settlement. Be careful when dealing with them as these adjusters are not on your side. You should refuse to give them a statement until you talk to us as your injury lawyers.

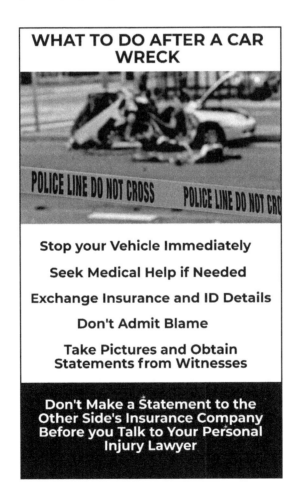

WHAT TO DO AFTER A CAR WRECK

POLICE LINE DO NOT CROSS   POLICE LINE DO NOT CRO

Stop your Vehicle Immediately

Seek Medical Help if Needed

Exchange Insurance and ID Details

Don't Admit Blame

Take Pictures and Obtain Statements from Witnesses

Don't Make a Statement to the Other Side's Insurance Company Before you Talk to Your Personal Injury Lawyer

CHAPTER 12

MEDICAL TREATMENT FOR YOUR INJURIES

The first thing you should do after any car accident is to seek the proper medical treatment for your injuries and obtain needed follow-up care. Initially, after a car accident, an ambulance will often arrive to take you to the emergency room. However, if you do not want to deal with an ambulance or an emergency room, you can follow-up with your own healthcare provider. You can also go to the hospital in a private car.

Regardless of how you seek medical attention, you should see a healthcare provider who can properly evaluate and treat your injuries. Aim to go to a healthcare provider that has treated you in the past since they are familiar with your past medical condition and they can render the proper medical treatment for your injuries. If you do not believe you were injured, there is no reason to seek any type of medical treatment but you may want to get checked out. Often, because of adrenalin and the stress of the situation, you may not know how hurt you are right away.

Depending on the severity of the motor vehicle accident, injuries can range from soft tissue-type injuries to the neck and back, broken bones, to nerve damage and internal injuries that require a multiple day stay at the hospital. A common injury from a motor vehicle collision is connective tissue injury to the spine area that can result when the initial collision causes a person to be bounced or thrown about in the car.

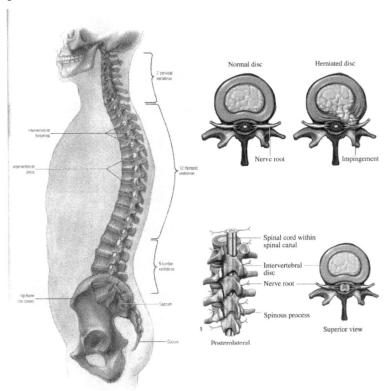

Normal disc

Herniated disc

Nerve root

Impingement

Spinal cord within spinal canal

Intervertebral disc

Nerve root

Spinous process

Superior view

Posterolateral

These types of injuries to muscles and tendons often harm the neck and back area. Injuries in the neck and back can involve the spinal cord, which runs from the base of the brain to the tailbone. The spine supports the body, allowing the body to remain upright, flex and twist. The spinal cord also acts like a large electrical cable with smaller cables, the nerves, running inside of it and branching out to the various extremities, the arms, the legs and the other parts of the body, somewhat like a tree and its branches.

The spine is constructed of bones known as vertebrae, and the vertebrae are wrapped with muscles and ligaments. The vertebrae are separated by discs, which are round shock absorber type structures, harder on the outside and softer on the inside. These discs allow proper spacing and cushion for the cervical spine and the lumbar spine.

Ligaments are bands of tissues that connect bones and hold them in place. The ligaments are injured when they get stretched. The muscles help move the spine. They can be injured when they are strained, sprained, or torn. These spinal injuries need proper medical attention to heal in the quickest way.

HEALTH INSURANCE COVERAGE

Use whatever health insurance is available to you when you get injured in a car accident. Many times healthcare providers will say you do not need to use your health insurance since the motor vehicle accident is not your fault. However, you should normally use all available healthcare coverage for all of your medical care for your injuries. This includes all visits to the hospital, to your main healthcare provider, physical therapy or chiropractic treatment and diagnostic testing.

Millions of Americans do not have health insurance coverage. If you are injured in a car accident and you lack health insurance, you should try to find a healthcare provider that will treat you even though you do not have health insurance coverage. An experienced injury lawyer will know which doctors will treat you even without health insurance – essentially on credit to be paid out of your case.

If you do not have health insurance, medical payments coverage, may be available to you from the car insurance policy, either from the vehicle you were riding in or your own personal car insurance policy.

The most important thing in any motor vehicle accident is to be sure you receive the proper medical treatment. Unfortunately, depending on the nature and the severity of the injuries, you can often treat for months and possibly even years. You can have permanent disability and chronic, long-term pain from a car accident.

Sometimes, nothing will bring you back to the way you were before the car accident, and that is why it is so important to receive the proper medical treatment to get you back to as close as possible to your health before the wreck.

CHAPTER 13

WHAT CAN I CLAIM AFTER A CAR ACCIDENT?

PROPERTY DAMAGE ISSUES

After a motor vehicle accident, not only do you have to deal with any injuries that you suffered, but you also have to deal with a car, truck, SUV or van that has been damaged because of the accident. The property damage caused in a car accident is inconvenient because you have to go without your car while it is getting repaired. Also, the defendant's insurance company only authorizes certain repairs which can fall well below your expectations. You may find the paint no longer matches or the vehicle is not running like before. Also, the defendant's insurance company could simply declare your vehicle a total loss and give you a check for the fair market value to the vehicle, which generally does not reflect the true value of your vehicle to you.

The defendant's insurance company can be difficult when you are trying to get your vehicle fixed. You are entitled to a rental vehicle while your car is being repaired, but the defendant's insurance can limit how many days you get a rental vehicle. It may be better to call your own insurance company to get the property damage fixed, but, again, then you have to pay your deductible and you may not get a rental vehicle unless you have rental coverage on your policy. Hopefully, you will get back your deductible in the future since your insurance company will go after the other insurance company for this money.

If you lack rental coverage on your car insurance policy, you may have no vehicle while your car is undergoing repairs. The laws in Virginia do not benefit the person who has the property damage and often you will feel treated poorly by the insurance company in the process. The defendant's insurance company generally does not go out of its way to properly fix the car or to fairly estimate the true value of your car. If we represent you in an injury case from the wreck, we hope to take some sting out of the process by doing enough good for you on the injury claim to make up for the raw deal you will likely get on the car damage.

LOST WAGES

Besides dealing with the property damage to your car, you may lose time from work because of your injuries. Unfortunately, these lost wages generally are not repaid until a much later date. There is no good solution to this problem other than looking to your own car insurance policy to see if you have coverage to help with the loss of wages because of a car accident. Most people do not have this coverage on their policy.

The defendant's insurance company generally will not pay you for lost wages unless you sign some type of release which will finalize and close your case. Your healthcare provider, typically, must provide a note to keep you out of work if you want the defendant's insurance company to consider your lost wages. The bottom line is that when you are injured and miss time from work, there is no quick solution and that this can greatly hamper paying the family bills and putting food on the table. Some lucky folks do have short-term disability policies or generous sick leave through work.

Severe injuries cause not only past lost wages but can involve future lost wages. Depending on the severity of the case, we may hire experts to prove your loss and compensate you properly. We may use a qualified physical therapist who will provide a functional capacity evaluation that will determine what permanent work restrictions you have because of your injuries. Vocational experts figure out what kinds of jobs you can still do, if any, within your physical limitations. At some point, we may need an economist to determine the present value for these future lost wages.

INJURIES: PAIN AND INCONVENIENCE

Pain and inconvienice after a car accident can be harder to handle than being faced with the property damage to your vehicle and the loss of wages. Ongoing pain and discomfort is typical after a car accident. Your pain will probably cause you difficulty getting out of bed in the morning, problems with your daily activities, and with sleeping.

Unfortunately, you generally cannot be compensated for your pain and inconvenience until you have totally finished your medical treatment. The defendant's insurance company may try to settle with you before you finish your treatment. People who accept this money sign away any rights they have in the future. The only thing that can help you get through this pain and inconvenience is making sure you have the proper medical treatment and then realizing that you have legal rights to protect you. Most people do not realize the staggering amount of inconvenience a motor vehicle accident causes because of the damage to the vehicle as well as the injuries that resulted from the accident. Basically, your whole life is disrupted and if you can be prepared for the difficulty at the beginning it makes this challenging process a little easier.

CHAPTER 14
MOTOR VEHICLE LAW IN VIRGINIA

GENERAL LAWS IN VIRGINIA INJURY CASES

These are some basic laws in Virginia relating to car accidents. There are two primary issues in any collision:

1. Who is at fault for the accident?

2. How much money should be awarded to you for your injuries?

The laws in Virginia that govern car accidents can be complicated. We referred to the issue of fault in Chapter 6. This is an overview of some of the relevant laws in Virginia without giving specific legal advice. The most important concept in Virginia car wreck law is negligence, which is a fancy lawyer word for who is at fault for the accident. The definition of negligence is the failure to use ordinary care. Ordinary care is defined as the care a reasonable person would use under similar facts and circumstances.

In Virginia, the person who is injured and is bringing the lawsuit is referred to as the plaintiff. The plaintiff has the burden of proving by the greater weight of the evidence that the defendant was at fault for the accident and the crash was also the cause of any injuries to the plaintiff.

Interestingly enough, the law in Virginia states that the fact that there was an accident does not necessarily mean that the injured plaintiff recovers money, since an accident may not be the fault of any particular person.

Virginia is one of the few states left in the country that follows the idea of contributory negligence as a complete bar to recovery. Contributory negligence is defined as the failure to act as a reasonable person would have acted for his own safety under the circumstances of the case. The law in Virginia states that if you are contributorily negligent in causing the wreck, you cannot recover any money for your injuries. This drastic law prevents you from recovering any money even if you are only 1 percent at fault for the accident and the defendant is 99 percent at fault for the accident. The defendant has the burden of proof to show that you are contributorily negligent in the accident.

The law in the Commonwealth states that if a judge or jury finds that both the plaintiff and the defendant were negligent, and the negligence of both caused or was a factor in the accident, you cannot compare the negligence of the parties. Any negligence of the plaintiff which was a "proximate or direct cause" of the accident will bar the plaintiff from recovering any money. This is an unbelievably harsh rule. Many people do not understand why Virginia has this rule of contributory negligence in regards to a motor vehicle accident, and really it is not fair but an old rule that needs to be changed. We are often asked if not wearing a seatbelt is contributory negligence. Although this may make injuries worse, it will not prevent you bringing a lawsuit.

The law in Virginia also talks about credibility of witnesses, which can greatly influence the outcome of your case. The law states that the judge or jury decides the credibility of witnesses and weighs up the believability of the testimony of these witnesses based on their appearance, the matter of the witnesses on the stand, their intelligence and any bias they have toward the case.

LAWS WHEN YOU DRIVE A MOTOR VEHICLE

In Virginia, the following laws help determine who is at fault in a motor vehicle accident. Every driver has a duty to keep a proper lookout, to keep his vehicle under proper control and to operate his vehicle at a reasonable speed. If the driver fails to perform any of these, he is at fault.

Also, the driver of a motor vehicle shall not follow another motor vehicle too closely. A driver who is following too closely if usually to blame for a rear-end collision.

An important law in Virginia is the duty to keep a lookout. Generally, the law states the duty to keep a proper lookout requires a driver to use ordinary care to look in all directions for vehicles, people or conditions that would affect his driving, to see what a reasonable person would have seen and to react as a reasonable person would have acted to avoid a collision.. Drivers who fail to keep a proper lookout are judged to be at fault for an accident.

Another law states that the maximum speed limit at the time and place of the collision is a key factor in determining negligence. If the defendant was driving his vehicle faster than this limit, he could be negligent in the particular accident. As such, simply going over the speed limit by 1 or 2 miles could prove a lack of due care.

a driver changes lanes, that motorist has a duty to drive within a single lane and not to move from that lane until he or she has checked it's safe to switch lanes.

Under Virginia law, a driver who is turning must give a signal to any vehicle that may be affected by his intended movement. It is crucial to use your blinkers when turning so that the vehicles around you know that you will be turning and in which direction.

Although a driver facing a green light can proceed, he or she has a duty to yield to other oncoming vehicles and pedestrians lawfully within the intersection. Also, in proceeding through the intersection, that driver has a duty to exercise ordinary care. If a driver fails to do either, one of these things, he is negligent. If a driver has a yellow light, the driver has a duty not to enter the intersections, including crosswalks, unless you cannot stop without causing a hazard. If he fails to do this, he is at fault.

At a stop sign, a driver has a duty to stop completely at a clearly marked stop line before entering any intersection. He has to yield to the right of way to any approaching vehicle. If a driver does not do this, he is at fault for any accident. Drivers do not have to stop by law at a yield sign unless another vehicle is approaching and has the right of way.

LAWS FOR DAMAGES IN VIRGINIA

Virginia allows an award of money if you are injured through no fault of your own in a motor vehicle accident. Unfortunately, there is no precise formula to determine the amount of damages. The judge or jury considers the following aspects to harms and losses in awarding damages in any personal injury matter:

1. Any bodily injury sustained and how these ~~injures~~ *injuries* affect your health according to the degree and duration;

2. Any physical pain and mental anguish suffered in the past or in the future;

3. Any scarring and any associated humiliation or embarrassment because of said scarring;

4. Any inconveniences caused in the past that are expected to be caused in the future;

5. Any medical expenses occurred in the past and any that may be caused in the future;

6. Any earnings lost;

7. Any lessening of earning capacity that may be reasonably expected to be sustained in the future; and

8. Any property damage.

The judge or jury considers all of the applicable elements in your case in coming to a proper award for the damages in your personal injury case. The person bringing the claim has the burden of proving each of the elements of the damages in their particular case.

The fact that you have health insurance to pay some of your bills does not decrease the amount of your award because the existence of health insurance is not allowed to be known to the jury which just considers the full amount of the medical bills in deciding the amount of damages. The monetary award should be based solely on the testimony and the evidence presented in the courtroom based on the above eight factors that apply.

PRE-EXISTING CONDITIONS
IN CAR ACCIDENT CASES

If the injured party had a condition before the accident that was aggravated because of the accident or a pre-existing condition that made the injury more severe or difficult to treat, the injured party may recover for the increased severity of difficulty of treatment. However, the injured party cannot recover for the pre-existing condition.

Extreme reckless negligence by the defendant gives you the right to be awarded punitive or additional damages in your case. The judge or jury can award punitive damages if the defendant acted with malice toward the plaintiff or acted under the circumstances amounting to willful and wanton disregard to plaintiff's rights, such as drunk driving by the defendant. However, punitive damages can only be awarded when:

- The blood/alcohol content of a drunk driver who caused a crash was 0.15 or greater at the time of the wreck.

- A drunk driver refused to to take a blood-alcohol test upon arrest.

- If the at-fault driver acted "with malice toward the victim or his or her conduct was so willful or wanton as to show a conscious disregard for the rights of others."

These damages are awarded to punish the defendant for his actions and to serve as an example to prevent others from acting in a similar way. The judge or jury specifically states that these damages are for punitive damages. The other damages for the harms and losses to you are often called compensatory damages, which are separate from punitive damages. Punitive damages are rarely allowed in Virginia, and cannot exceed a certain amount by law.

CHAPTER 15
HOW TO HIRE A LAWYER

HOW DO I DECIDE WHICH LAWYER TO HIRE FOR MY PERSONAL INJURY CLAIM?

There are many factors that go into hiring an attorney for your personal injury case. In picking a personal injury attorney, the following factors should be considered:

1. You want to hire a lawyer who practices primarily in the field of personal injury law. Not all firms focus on accidents and injuries. Ours does 100 percent. You want a lawyer who specializes in injury cases, not someone who is just dabbling. The at-fault driver's insurance company knows who the attorneys are that will go to court and try the cases and they use this information in evaluating your claim.

2. Many times you can ask a family member or friend if they know of an attorney that handles personal injury matters as it is always important to try to have some type of comfort level with whatever attorney you choose. You can check out our videos at CooperHurley.com to "meet" us and get a preview of what we are about.

3. Experience matters. Both Jim Hurley and John Cooper have been injury lawyers for decades. Also, it is important to pick an attorney with experience not only in the practice of

personal injury law but also an attorney that has experience in litigation cases.

4. Cooper Hurley Injury Lawyers has a great reputation for legal knowledge and ethics as we are rated AV by Martindale Hubbell/Lawyers.com. We are recognized by other bodies such as the Million Dollar Advocates forum for winning cases worth more than $1 million. You want someone recognized in the law field as a highly experienced injury lawyer.

After choosing an attorney, it is important to be sure you understand how that attorney and his or her office operates in regards to a personal injury matter. Your attorney should explain at the beginning what to expect during the course of representation.

WHY WON'T A LAWYER TAKE MY CASE OR WHY DID MY LAWYER STOP REPRESENTING ME?

Sometimes a personal injury attorney will not take your case or will stop representing you and you do not understand why. Some common reasons for personal injury attorneys to decline representation or stop representing you on your personal injury are the following:

1. Minor injuries that do not warrant the time and effort from the lawyer's standpoint.

2. A possibility that you are partially at fault for the accident since that might totally preclude you from getting any money.

3. Having had a prior lawyer represent you in this matter because many lawyers do not like to jump in mid-way to try to resolve a personal injury matter.

4. If you have unrealistic expectations, sometimes an attorney may sense you probably will not be happy with any likely result.

5. The failure to listen to your lawyer's advice on your case, which can severely affect the outcome of your matter.

In choosing a personal injury attorney to represent you for your injuries, it is important that you feel comfortable with both the attorney and the staff so you are satisfied with the process and the resolution to your case. Any personal injury attorney wants his client to have a successful outcome and be happy with his services. Unfortunately, there are times when a personal injury attorney simply cannot satisfy you, so you must try to understand your particular case from the attorney's point of view as well. Even the best attorney cannot change the law and the facts.

Your decision on who to hire as your accident lawyer is a big one. You can shop around. Our lawyers will talk with you without charge and with no obligation. We trust you'll pick us because we are experienced, specialized, trustworthy and friendly. Once you chat with us, we hope and expect you will want us to help you with your accident case.

CHAPTER 16

WHAT COOPER HURLEY INJURY LAWYERS WILL DO FOR YOU

Your life may be turned upside down by a car accident. You don't know who to turn to. Dealing directly with an insurance company carries inherent risks. By hiring an attorney, you take on someone who is on your side. Our job at Cooper Hurley Injury Lawyers is to protect your legal rights when you are injured in a car accident. Our firm practices almost exclusively in representing people who are hurt in motor vehicle accidents. We also file wrongful death cases for family members of people who died in car accidents. We will assist you in every single phase of the legal process. Your job is to get better from the injuries you suffered because of the motor vehicle accident.

Cooper Hurley Injury Lawyers can do the following to assist you after a motor vehicle accident:

1. **Initial Interview:** Immediately talk with you so that you know what to expect during the course of our representation of you.

2. **Gather Information:** Gather all information including police accident reports, medical records, witness statements, diagrams of the accident scene and all initial investigation matters.

3. **Examine Insurance Coverage**: Part of our job is to determine what insurance is available including from the at-fault driver. We will always ask you to provide us with your information, so we can look at your coverage to see if you can or should use your insurance coverage to maximize your recovery. We will recommend any changes to your current insurance policy which should help protect you in the future.

4. **Review All Legal Issues:** Research and examine all the legal aspects of your case like contributory negligence, punitive damages, and all other legal theories that may affect the outcome of your case.

5. **Gather All Medical Information:** During the course of your treatment, we will gather your medical records, medical bills and, if necessary, discuss with your doctor any permanent problems you may have as a result of your injuries.

6. **Negotiate Your Case With Your Input**: After gathering all of your medical records, medical bills, lost wage information and doing a thorough investigation of your case, we assemble and send your information to the defendant's insurance company so that we can begin negotiating your claim. After getting first a number from the defendant's insurance company, we will contact you and discuss their offer. We will give your our advice and legal opinions on whether your case should settle or whether litigation should be pursued. Settling the case is your call. We just give you our experienced advice, but we only act with your permission.

7. **Litigation If Needed:** If we decide that the settlement offer is unfair and that litigation is appropriate, Cooper Hurley Injury Lawyers will file a lawsuit. After getting a trial date, we will do everything to prepare your case – getting witnesses ready for the trial, preparing the exhibits, and organizing all aspects for your trial. We will try your case in front of a judge or a jury so that you can get an award that would reflect the injuries and the pain you suffered from this motor vehicle accident. Often cases settle before trial, as we show the insurer that we are ready for trial.

Besides helping you with the above items, Cooper Hurley Injury Lawyers will also protect your interests by helping you in these areas.

If you have serious injuries, it may be helpful to determine permanent impairment ratings or prepare a life care plan, which shows what you will need in the way of medicine, therapists, in home-health rehabilitation, or medical equipment for the rest of your life. Experts are usually needed to determine a permanent disability rating and the financial effects that disability may have. In cases that involve serious injury and permanent disability, the jury must understand the continued expense of treating these injuries and how they will affect you for the rest of your life. If your injuries are so severe that you cannot return to your former job or cannot return to work at all, you may be able to recover damages for the loss of future earing capacity. We will need experts, such as a vocational rehabilitation counselor and an economist, to help you establish the amount of wages lost and your future lost earning capacity because of the severity of your injuries.

Sometimes when there is a substantial settlement, a structured settlement is often in your best interests. A structured settlement provides a stream of guaranteed tax-free payments but has drawbacks. The structured settlement essentially defers income so that you can have yearly or monthly income for a certain period of time, even rest of your life. There are tax implications to structured settlements so that must be kept in mind to make sure the structured settlement is done properly. If you are talking hundreds of thousands of dollars or millions of dollars, a structured settlement or a partial structured settlement can be an attractive way to help resolve your matter. The choice of whether to have a structured settlement is always yours.

CHAPTER 17
TIPS TO HELP YOUR CASE

Here are our top ten best bits of advice to help you regarding any injury that you receive because of a motor vehicle accident that is not your fault:

Tip #1: Seek needed treatment immediately. The best thing you can do is seek immediate treatment for all injuries from a motor vehicle accident. You may want to try to go to your family doctor or a doctor that has seen you in the past since they are familiar with you. It is also important to remember that prompt medical care will help you get better, but it also shows the pain and suffering because of your injuries. Please follow through with your medical treatment. Do not miss appointments, or decide on your own that you are better. It is always important to follow through with your medical treatment until your healthcare provider releases you from treatment.

Tip #2: Don't rush to settle your case quickly. Typically, the defendant's insurance company will wave a few thousand dollars in front of your nose immediately after the accident to settle your claim. If you've been injured in a motor vehicle accident, it is important to remember that the defendant's insurance company is not your friend. At first, this offer may seem particularly attractive because you need money right away, but what you may not realize is, when you sign a release, then you are waiving your legal rights to any other or further money. Without legal representation, it is difficult to understand what your options are, which further shows that, on any significant personal injury that you suffer, it is wise to have a personal injury attorney protect your best interests. Generally speaking, settling your case quickly does not allow you to be fully compensated for any medical bills, pain and suffering, or lost wages, especially if the injury is permanent; it only benefits the insurance company. You do not want to settle the case one day and to learn later you need surgery.

Tip #3: Do not underestimate the defendant's insurance adjusters who contact you. Initially, after a motor vehicle accident when you are injured, if you are not represented by a lawyer, the defendant's insurance adjuster will call you and try to entice you to settle your claim. The insurance adjuster will often act like your friend and claim to seek to help you out, but remember even though they may be extremely pleasant, their only goal is to convince you to settle your claim as quickly and cheaply as possible. These adjusters do this day in and day out and, unfortunately, these insurance company adjusters are skilled at persuading you not to hire a lawyer. The adjuster will often tell you that you do not need a lawyer since you can deal with the insurance company on your own. You may choose to deal directly with an insurance company if there's a minor injury or a minor accident; however, in anything but a minor injury with a minor accident, having a lawyer greatly increases the likelihood of a fair recovery for your particular matter.

Tip #4: Do not provide a statement to the defendant's insurance adjuster because this could hurt your case. You never have to give a recorded statement and should refuse to do so. It is fine to talk to the insurance adjuster about the property damage to your vehicle but do not discuss your injuries. You can simply tell the adjuster that your attorney on the injury case will provide all information about your injuries. If you do give a statement, you may say something that hurts your case down the road. Even just friendly questions about how you are feeling are intended to probe you for medical information. Often the insurance adjuster will immediately contact you and try to get a statement, just say your attorney told you no to do so.

Tip #5: The defendant's insurance adjuster often will request that you sign medical authorizations forms so they can get all your health records. You do not want to do this as it allows the defendant's insurance adjuster to invade your privacy and to look for past medical problems that may or may not be related to this particular accident. It is important to contact a lawyer to protect your rights. Your injury lawyer can collect the needed records for you.

Tip #6: Start a file and write down everything about your case. Please be sure to put everything in that file so that it is all together. Besides documenting anything about how the accident happened, you want to keep copies of records that could be important to your case. Obviously, if you have an attorney, share all this data with your counsel.

Tip #7: Honesty is always the best policy. Be honest when you are dealing with injuries. If you are not injured, there is no need to go to a healthcare provider. You want to be clear and truthful about the accident and injuries with all doctors. Even little errors or inconsistencies may be blown up into "lies" by the insurance lawyers.

Tip #8: If you do hire a lawyer, be sure to tell your lawyer everything. People will occasionally try to hide things from their lawyer, thinking that it will help their case. It is important to be honest with your lawyer. Your attorney will keep your information confidentially, and work through any difficult problems with you. If we know all the facts, we can best deal with any problems together.

Tip #9: Only hire an attorney who devotes all of his practice to personal injury cases. The key is that you want to have a lawyer who regularly practices this particular type of law. A lawyer who does not constantly practice in this particular area simply will not have the day in and day out experience to best help you against the insurance company and defense lawyers. All you need to do is look at the lawyer's website or ask a few questions and you will know if this lawyer specializes in accident law and has enough experience to know what they are doing.

Explaining the Car Accident injury process

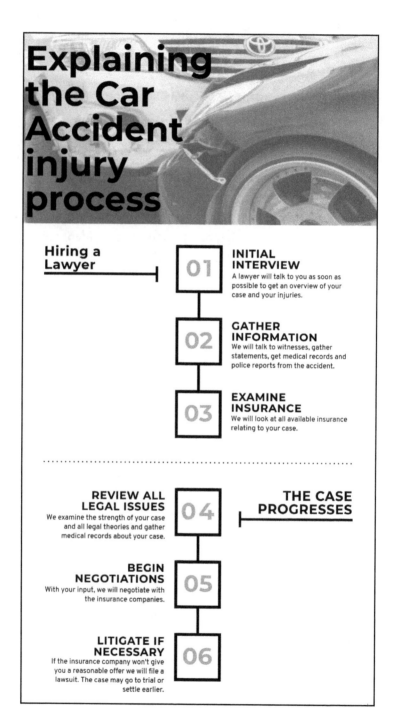

Hiring a Lawyer

01
INITIAL INTERVIEW
A lawyer will talk to you as soon as possible to get an overview of your case and your injuries.

02
GATHER INFORMATION
We will talk to witnesses, gather statements, get medical records and police reports from the accident.

03
EXAMINE INSURANCE
We will look at all available insurance relating to your case.

04
REVIEW ALL LEGAL ISSUES
We examine the strength of your case and all legal theories and gather medical records about your case.

THE CASE PROGRESSES

05
BEGIN NEGOTIATIONS
With your input, we will negotiate with the insurance companies.

06
LITIGATE IF NECESSARY
If the insurance company won't give you a reasonable offer we will file a lawsuit. The case may go to trial or settle earlier.

CHAPTER 18

LITIGATION: WHAT DOES IT MEAN TO FILE A LAWSUIT?

In some cases, the injury claim will not settle because the insurance company refuses to offer an amount of money that is fair based on injuries. The goal of the insurance company is to pay as little as they can to you for your injuries.

As such, you may need to file a lawsuit in your case so as to recover a reasonable sum for your injuries suffered in the motor vehicle accident. A lawsuit can be a difficult and complicated matter. Fortunately, the attorneys at Cooper Hurley Injury Lawyers file personal injury lawsuits on a regular basis and are set up to deal with all aspects of the lawsuit so as to protect your rights under the circumstances.

Filing a lawsuit for a personal injury matter without a lawyer in Virginia is extremely difficult and risky and often results in a bad outcome. If your personal injury may require a lawsuit, it is wise to consider hiring a personal injury attorney who practices and litigates in this area to help you with your case.

Virginia has two courts for lawsuits involving a personal injury. The first court is small claims court, General District Court. If you have a minor injury, you can bring your case to small claims court for a judge to decide your case. In Virginia, there is no jury in small claims court, and you can sue for an amount up to

$25,000 for any injuries you suffered. In small claims court, it is difficult to proceed without a personal injury attorney because the defendant generally has an attorney hired by his insurance company. Without an attorney, there are many traps that you could fall into to ruin your case. As such, even on legitimate smaller cases, it is important to have a lawyer to protect your best interests.

The majority of personal injury cases are filed in Circuit Court. In Circuit Court, you can sue for any amount you choose, even millions of dollars, based on the nature and severity of your injuries. However, any suit filed in Circuit Court is a major undertaking for both the lawyer and yourself. These lawsuits take one to two years to come to trial from the time that these lawsuits are filed. The majority of people do not understand the delay from the date of the filing of the lawsuit until a trial date, but the personal injury lawyer must do many things between the date you file the lawsuit and the date of the trial in regards to your case.

In the Circuit Court, the first thing is to file the lawsuit. The next phase is the discovery phase, where Interrogatories and Requests for Production of Documents are sent to the other side. The Interrogatories are written questions requiring answers to provide details of what exactly happened on the day of the accident, the damages, and any other related matters. After answering this discovery, the defendant's attorney will send out legal documents to get your past medical records and any medical records associated with the accident. After the defendant's attorney reviews all these documents and your answers, depositions will usually happen next.

Depositions are face-to-face questions and answers in a lawyer's office when the other attorney asks you, in even more detail, what happened and what type of injuries you have. There is a court reporter present to record all questions and answers. The depositions are crucial in your case and you need to have your personal injury attorney prepare you for the defendant's attorney's questions as this process could severely impact the outcome of your case. Also, your attorney will ask the defendant various questions about how the accident happened so as to establish what occurred on that particular day and to be sure there are no surprises at trial. After the depositions, generally speaking, both sides will order the depositions and there will be a written record of that particular question and answer period.

After filing a lawsuit, finishing discovery, and taking depositions, a trial is the last step in a Virginia injury lawsuit. In Circuit Court accident cases the decision is usually made by a jury.

A personal injury attorney who litigates a case will spend days preparing your case and incur thousands (or tens of thousands) of dollars in expenses to be sure everything goes according to plan so as to present the facts and circumstances of your case in a favorable light.

Before your trial date, both sides will often suggest mediation to try to resolve your particular matter. In some cases, a court will order mediation or a settlement conference.

Dispute resolution though mediation can help save time and money by getting a settlement before trial. This is a method of non-binding dispute resolution involving a neutral third party, generally a retired judge, who tries to help the parties reach a mutually agreeable solution. Mediation is often used to bring the parties closer to a resolution and can, at times, completely solve the issues. At other times, it helps lead to a final resolution of your case at a later time, after the mediation conference but before trial.

During the litigation process, your attorney will typically continue to attempt settlement negotiations to arrive at a settlement value for your case that would be reasonable under the circumstances. Negotiation can happen at any time, even after trial starts.

Your attorney should know what he is doing so that he can properly prepare you and give you the proper expectations of how your litigation case may work out. Unfortunately, litigation is a last resort in resolving your case but, because of the attitude of many insurance companies, litigation may be the only way to help properly resolve your case for an amount of money that would be fair under the circumstances and acceptable to you.

Juries in Virginia tend to be conservative but will award good verdicts for cases that they think are about legitimate injuries. That is why it is important to have a lawyer to navigate this difficult labyrinth, and present your case in the best light.

Personal injury attorneys do not represent you for free. Typically, a personal injury attorney will represent you on a contingency fee basis. A contingency fee is a fee charged only if the lawsuit is successful or is favorably settled out of court. Contingency fees are usually calculated as a percentage of the client's gross recovery and are typically one-third (33 1/3%) before any type of significant work in regards to litigation and is often times higher if it does require litigation.

Most personal injury attorneys will advance or pay up front for you the costs in your case if they have a reasonable expectation that these will he repaid at some point. The client repays the lawyer after there is a successful result in the lawsuit or if the case is settled out of court. You do not pay if we do not secure a result. The attorney will draw up a contract with you when you sign up which will detail the terms of your representation.

The bottom line is, if you need to litigate your case, you want to hire an experienced, specialized car accident lawyer who will make sure you are properly prepared and have the necessary expectations to achieve a successful outcome.

CHAPTER 19

COOPER HURLEY INJURY LAWYER CAR ACCIDENT RESULTS

The attorneys at Cooper Hurley Injury Lawyers have achieved hundreds of verdicts and settlements in car accident cases. They include the following:

$5 MILLION FOR HAMPTON WOMAN HIT BY A CONSTRUCTION TRUCK

A terrifying crash with a construction truck on an unmarked road in Gloucester County left a woman from Hampton, Virginia, with severe injuries that changed her life.

The woman was driving on the narrow road when the truck came into her lane and crashed into her car. The impact was so intense that her car's engine was thrown onto her lap, causing multiple fractures and organ damage. At the age of 41, the woman suffered extensive rib fractures, liver laceration, a pelvic fracture, a fractured femur and right tibia as well as other injuries. Her symptoms also included post-traumatic stress disorder and mild traumatic brain injury.

The mother of the lady in the wreck had been a satisfied client of Jim Hurley in the past. When she contacted Cooper Hurley Injury Lawyers, we realized that her daughter would need lifelong help with medical and living expenses. After getting the family's permission, we quickly filed a lawsuit against the at-fault driver and the construction company that employed him in the Newport News Circuit Court.

Our client ended up with amnesia after the crash. Fortunately, an eyewitness in a car behind our client's identified himself to the police and told investigators the truck came into our client's lane. Physical evidence at the scene confirmed this fact. To preserve this key evidence we took the deposition of this eyewitness immediately.

The worker was using a company vehicle and we were able to prove that he was acting within the scope of his employment. This was an important finding because it meant we could sue the construction company. John Cooper managed to get the truck operator's cell phone records that showed he was on the phone close to the time of the wreck. We were able to force the insurance company defense lawyers to admit liability, although they wanted to say that the road was the cause of the crash because of its curve and its narrowness.

Injury attorneys, John Cooper and Jim Hurley, were working as fast as possible getting the case ready for trial. Our client was struggling for months to function day to day and needed a walker. She initially required eight hours a day of in-home help to assist with the daily living activities she had previously taken for granted. Our staff stayed in constant touch with the client and her husband to help make sure all the treatment that was needed was given.

When the time was right, we met with the patient's main surgeon, to get him to document the harms and losses from her injuries. An orthopedic evaluation under the American Medical

LAWYERS WEEKLY
VIRGINIA

| Vol. 30, No. 45 | valawyersweekly.com |

VERDICTS & SETTLEMENTS

Mild brain injury caused by rear-ender

$150,000 Settlement

COOPER

O'HANLON

The plaintiff was the driver of a motor vehicle that was stopped at a red traffic light. A pick-up truck operated by the defendant collided with the rear of the plaintiff's vehicle. The defendant claimed at the accident scene that he suffered a medical emergency. The defendant did have a syncopal event caused by a previously undiagnosed heart problem. The defendant had a history of fainting but recently had been cleared to drive by his Navy doctor.

Following the collision, the plain- tiff presented to emergency medical personnel with complaints of confusion/amnesia, nausea and loss of consciousness, along with surgical and thoracic pain. The plaintiff was ultimately diagnosed with a mild traumatic brain injury as a result of the wreck.

[16-T-047]

Type of action:	Personal Injury - Motor Vehicle
Injuries alleged:	Mild traumatic brain injury and connective tissue injuries
Court:	Virginia Beach Circuit Court
Date resolved:	Feb. 1, 2016
Verdict or settlement:	Settlement
Amount:	$150,000.00
Attorneys for plaintiff:	John M. Cooper and Griffin M. O'Hanlon, Norfolk

Association's guidelines found she was left with a permanent 58 percent impairment of her body. That might not mean much to the lay person, but it meant her life was severely affected by the accident. She would be suffering chronic pain that required daily medication and would have life-long restricted mobility requiring the use of a cane.

In cases like this, we are always acutely aware of the potential effects of a brain injury that can permanently change the life of someone who has been involved in a car wreck. The mild traumatic brain injury claim was hotly contested by the attorneys representing the truck driver's insurance company. Mild traumatic brain injuries can be tricky to diagnose and nobody identified it until we sent our client to see a neuropsychiatrist. Evidence of post-traumatic stress disorder was clearer to the doctors who treated our client from the outset. She frequently had nightmares about the wreck.

John Cooper and Jim Hurley had prepared the evidence for trial and showed it to non-lawyers to see how they would react to the case. These focus groups, which included a neutral presentation of the facts to two different sets of jurors, were vital to figuring out the real value of the claim. The results of the mock deliberations were videoed and were ready to send to the attorneys for the insurance company, if needed. In significant cases that involve injuries as severe as these, it's important to go the extra mile for a client.

OUTCOME

We forced the insurers for the at-fault driver and company to settle for $5 million. The case took only 15 months from the time of the wreck to be successfully mediated, which is a relatively speedy resolution, given the complexity. We made sure that our client's future needs were taken care of.

OVER $2.86 MILLION FOR A DOUBLE AMPUTEE INJURED BY A DRUNK DRIVER

A 19-year-old highway worker was putting down cones out of a construction company vehicle on the I-264 in Norfolk in the early hours of the morning, when a drunk driver suddenly and unexpectedly veered around the traffic cones and a police cruiser with flashing blue lights and crashed into the back of the highway work crew's flatbed truck.

The young man was sitting on the edge of the truck with his legs dangling over the edge with a co-worker, when he was hit by the car at a high speed. The impact was so severe, he subsequently ended up losing both of his legs at the hospital. One leg was amputated above the knee and the other below the knee. One amputation is tough but two was a terrible injury to recover from.

Our client faced an uphill battle in rebuilding his life. His mother gave up her job to care for him and he learned to walk again over a period of months with the help of prosthetic legs and crutches. The severely hurt man sought a lawyer to file a lawsuit against the insurance policy of the drunk driver who was later convicted of a DUI. The young man and his family decided they wanted a law firm that concentrated on personal injury work, so he hired Cooper Hurley Injury Lawyers.

A personal injury case was filed by John Cooper in Norfolk Circuit Court and a workers' compensation claim was pursued with the Virginia Workers' Compensation Commission through co-counsel selected by Cooper Hurley Injury Lawyers.

VIRGINIA LAWYERS WEEKLY

Vol. 32, No. 52   valawyersweekly.com

_____VERDICTS & SETTLEMENTS_____

Man hurt arm, shoulder in accident with truck

$500,000 Settlement

HURLEY

O'MARA

BAKER

The plaintiff was traveling home when he struck a pick-up truck that attempted a left turn into his path in the Pungo area of Virginia Beach. The plaintiff suffered a serious shoulder and brachial plexus nerve injury resulting in a significant loss of function to his right arm.

Trial was scheduled prior to the plaintiff's military medical boards. In anticipation of an expected medical separation from the Navy, a vocational expert projected the plaintiff's loss of earning capacity to be in excess of $800,000.

While the plaintiff's injuries were mostly undisputed, liability was initially contested. While the speed limit at the intersection where the collision occurred was 45 mph, the plaintiff had just exited a construction zone with a cautionary

Type of action:	Personal Injury-Motorcycle Accident
Injuries alleged:	Right upper extremity brachial plexus nerve injury
Court:	Virginia Beach Circuit Court
Name of mediator:	Hon. Bradford Stillman (Ret.)
Date resolved:	Feb. 21, 2018
Special damages:	Medical Specials: $125,619.93; Loss of Earning Capacity: $800,000+
Demand:	$500,000 policy limits
Offer:	$500,000
Verdict or settlement:	Settlement
Amount:	$500,000
Attorneys for plaintiff:	Jim Hurley, Bill O'Mara and John Baker, Norfolk

speed limit of 40 mph. The accident report indicated that the plaintiff was traveling 45 mph before the crash. Two favorable independent witnesses were subsequently located and testified that the plaintiff appeared to be traveling at a safe speed.

The liability insurance carrier tendered its $500,000 policy limits the afternoon before mediation.

[18-T-046]

The workers' compensation system is good in that it guarantees some payment when Virginia workers get hurt on the job for a limited amount of lost wages and future medical bills. The problem is that it does not fully and fairly compensate people with injuries as great as those in this case as they get nothing for pain and suffering and other real harms and losses.

The loss of this young man's legs greatly decreased his potential to earn income. His lawyers hired a number of experts including a life care planner, an economist and an expert in physical medicine and rehabilitation to make a powerful case for compensation for his serious injuries. We also met with the key doctors of the patient to be sure we fully understood his medical and vocational situation.

Our client learned to walk again on artificial limbs. The double amputee never gave up on life. He also took up sports such as running and basketball, joining other men with handicaps. A desire to better himself led our client to enroll in a college course just over two years after the accident. Despite his upbeat attitude, his challenges meant he required money to purchase equipment to help make his home more handicap accessible and keep some quality of life. The man learned to drive with artificial legs, using an adapted vehicle.

OUTCOME

John Cooper and Jim Hurley of Cooper Hurley Injury Lawyers convinced the insurers for the at-fault driver to pay $936,775, all of the available insurance including under-insured motorist insurance for the drunk driver's actions. Our client was separately awarded an additional $1,930,000 in his workers' compensation claim, making a total of about $2.86 million. The workers' compensation amount was reached after a mediation with his past employer's insurer and was approved by Workers' Compensation Commission after presentation of information about the client's future medical needs.

We were happy to get this client's life back on track and to fight for him when he needed help most. Attorney John Cooper praised the young man's "resilience and positive outlook" as an inspiration to others. The funds made available to the client should ensure good financial security to take care of his own needs for the rest of his life.

$1.15 MILLION SETTLEMENT FOR A MOTHER AND DAUGHTER HURT IN AN EASTERN SHORE T-BONE CRASH

An 83-year-old mother and her 66-year-old daughter were trying to make a left turn from Route 13 in Northampton County on the Eastern Shore of Virginia.

As they made the maneuver, a car ran a red light at the intersection causing a T-bone collision. Side impact collisions are known as T-bone crashes or broadside accidents. Injuries sustained are often more serious because the sides of automobiles afford less protection.

Both women were knocked unconscious by the impact of the crash. The mother was transported to Riverside Shore Memorial Hospital on the Eastern Shore where she remained for 12 days. The daughter was airlifted from the accident scene to Riverside Regional Medical Center in Newport News. She remained at the hospital for nine days.

The mother required arm surgery. She suffered a fractured right arm and rib and suffered a concussion from the accident.

Her daughter sustained a fractured pelvis, arm and shoulder blade, as well as a subdural hematoma (brain bleed) as a result of this serious Eastern Shore T-bone crash.

The mother and daughter hired attorneys, John Cooper and Bill O'Mara of Cooper Hurley Injury Lawyers, who filed a personal injury lawsuit in Northampton County Circuit Court.

The defense team argued contributory negligence on behalf of the mother during the wreck. The daughter's orthopedic injuries did not require surgery or significant ongoing medical care and no future medical expenses were claimed for these injuries.

The defendant could not contest the wreck caused the subdural hematoma which is a collection of blood between the covering of the brain (dura) and the surface of the brain caused by a head injury. Other traumatic brain injury events before and after the crash complicated the neurosurgical evidence. The insurance defense attorneys fought damages claimed for the daughter's traumatic brain injury.

OUTCOME

An agreement was reached at a mediation involving attorneys John Cooper and Bill O'Mara just over five months before a trial date. The mother and daughter were awarded $1.15 million. The mother received $525,000 and the daughter $625,000. The settlement included special damages of $117,000 for the mother's medical bills and $101,000 for the daughter's medical bills.

VIRGINIA
LAWYERS WEEKLY

Vol. 32, No. 8   valawyersweekly.com

——————VERDICTS & SETTLEMENTS——————

Death settlement limited by defendant's limits, UIM

$1 Million Settlement

COOPER

The decedent was a beloved daughter and sister who was killed in a car crash as a passenger when her vehicle was rear ended by a drunken driver in Norfolk on April 24, 2016. The collision occurred at the intersection of E. Princess Anne Road and Sewells Point Road. The statutory beneficiaries in the wrongful death case included the mother, father, a brother and several half brothers and sisters.

The decedent's family was from Maryland so the plaintiff's counsel had a Virginia investigator appointed as administrator as required under Virginia law. The underinsured motorist negotiations included a resolution by agreement of the companion cases of the young woman's fiancé's case and another friend who was also in the automobile with them.

The total amount of the settlement was limited by the amount of insurance which was primarily UIM through the victim's family policy.

The young woman who died had been a talented athlete at Virginia Wesleyan College in Virginia Beach and was finishing her first year as a medical student at Eastern Virginia Medical School in Norfolk. The tragedy for the family and the community was devastating.

Type of action:	Wrongful Death
Name of case:	Rod Budd, Administrator of the Estate of Nancy Kelly, Deceased v. Thomas Walters
Court:	Norfolk Circuit Court
Case no.:	CL17-0207
Date resolved:	July 5, 2017
Special damages:	$6,000 in funeral expenses and $40,000 in hospital emergency room services
Demand:	$1,000,000
Offer:	$1,000,000
Verdict or settlement:	Settlement
Amount:	$1,000,000
Attorney for plaintiff:	John M. Cooper, Norfolk
Insurance carrier:	GEICO and Encompass

The at-fault driver was subject to punitive damages because he was intoxicated at the time of the crash. However, the defendant had only minimum insurance in the Commonwealth of Virginia which is $25,000 per person, $50,000 per accident. In addition to our client's vehicle, the crash involved another vehicle too.

Resolution of the case took place shortly after the conviction of the defendant on the DUI charges and sentencing.

[17-T-107]

$1 MILLION SETTLEMENT FOR FAMILY OF PASSENGER KILLED BY DRUNK DRIVER IN HAMPTON ROADS

A passenger lost her life when the car she was traveling in was rear-ended at an intersection in Hampton Roads by a DUI driver.

The young woman was a talented collegiate athlete and had a promising medical career ahead of her at the time she was involved in the car crash. The driver who hit her was found to be drunk at the scene of the wreck. Another vehicle was also involved in the crash.

Attorney John Cooper filed a wrongful death lawsuit on behalf of the woman's mother, father, a brother, and several half brothers and sisters.

The underinsured motorist (UIM) negotiations in the case included a resolution by agreement of the companion cases of the young woman's fiancé's case and another friend who was also in the car with them at the time of the wreck. The total amount of the settlement was limited by the amount of insurance which was primarily the underinsured motorist insurance through the victim's family policy.

The at-fault driver was subject to punitive damages because he was found to be intoxicated at the time of the crash. However, the defendant had only minimum insurance in the Commonwealth of Virginia which is $25,000 per person, $50,000 per accident.

Resolution of the case took place shortly after the at-fault driver was sentenced for the DUI.

VIRGINIA LAWYERS WEEKLY

Vol. 33, No. 20   valawyersweekly.com

VERDICTS & SETTLEMENTS

Driver claimed injuries caused by pre-existing conditions

$343,915 Settlement

COOPER

BAKER

Type of action:	Personal Injury
Injuries alleged:	Torn Rotator Cuff, Fractured Elbow, Neck Injury
Name of mediator:	Hon. Von L. Piersall (Ret.)
Date resolved:	Aug. 21, 2018
Special damages:	Over $120,000.00 claimed in medical bills, $16,000.00 in lost wages
Verdict or settlement:	Settlement
Amount:	$343,915
Attorneys for plaintiff:	John M. Cooper and John Baker, Norfolk

Plaintiff suffered serious injuries when she was struck by a driver who failed to yield and broadsided her. There was modest property damage to plaintiff's car and minimal to defendant's SUV. The defendant, a college student, at first blamed the wreck on a bus blocking his view and claimed the bus driver waved him out. Eventually this defense was dropped after depositions and requests for admission.

The plaintiff's medical treatment was extensive though she did not go to emergency room or seek care until days after the wreck. Plaintiff's orthopedist eventually did an arthroscopic shoulder surgery. Plaintiff had had advanced rheumatoid arthritis and osteo-arthritis for years before the crash. The operation on the partial thickness tear also addressed synovitis and bony anatomical features that were pre-existing. The elbow compression fracture developed late and may have been caused by the use of a dynamic splint as part of post-surgical therapy. Defense counsel argued that plaintiff had significant, symptomatic pre-existing medical conditions which were the cause of her pain and impairments. The defense medical examiner, Dr. John Aldridge, claimed that none of the care was accident related, not even the surgery. The case was settled at a judicial settlement conference within the month before trial. [18-T-114]

The claim included $6,000 in funeral expenses and $40,000 in hospital emergency room services.

OUTCOME

The case was resolved before trial by settlement for $1 million.

$815,000 FOR YOUNG MAN HIT BY A RED LIGHT RUNNER IN VIRGINIA BEACH

A pick-up truck driver ran a red light at the intersection of Independence Boulevard and Virginia Beach Boulevard in Virginia Beach. He hit a car driven by a 21-year-old man from the Eastern Shore of Virginia, who sustained a likely concussion that left him dazed at the accident scene.

The main chronic injury to the young man was a permanent traumatic brain injury that caused him to suffer almost constant headaches as well as cognitive impairments and anxiety. He also sustained knee, arm and neck injuries that healed. His family hired John Cooper and Jim Hurley of Cooper Hurley Injury Lawyers because of a referral from another attorney. The lawsuit was filed in Virginia Beach Circuit Court.

The accident dramatically impacted the young man's career plans. It meant he was no longer able to pursue a planned career as a truck driver which he was just starting out on. Instead he is now working as a store clerk with a kind employer who accommodated his challenges. Our client had his earning capacity as a worker reduced by $10,000 to $20,000 a year, according to a vocational expert hired by Cooper Hurley Injury Lawyers.

The pick-up truck driver was forced by our lawyers to admit fault, though he tried to make excuses at the scene. During a deposition, we established that he falsely claimed to police at the accident scene that brake failure caused the accident.

The nature and the extent of the young man's head injuries played an important part in the attack made by the insurance companies defending the pick-up truck driver. Brain injuries are often permanent in nature and can require lifelong care. Doctors hired by the insurance company admitted our client had a concussion, but said it must have healed within six weeks of the accident. Hired guns for the defense claimed any ongoing symptoms were from malingering, exaggeration and faking. Experts hired by Cooper Hurley Injury Lawyers said the effects of the injuries were real, ongoing and would significantly impact our client's future.

The family of the injured man, including his mother and step-father, as well as his employer, would have also been called to explain the permanent problems to the jury. The crux of a traumatic brain injury case is often the credibility of the claimant. We established that our client was a formerly happy and healthy guy who struggled to live a productive life, even to just hold down a job.

OUTCOME

The lawyers convinced the insurers to pay $815,000 during mediation. The case was settled about 45 days before it was due to go to trial. The client was pleased that we believed in him and glad to have a nest egg to fall back on if he needed it.

These are just some of the cases won by Cooper Hurley Injury Lawyers. All cases are unique and different and no previous result is an indicator of a future result.

LAWYERS WEEKLY
VIRGINIA

Vol. 31, No. 24   valawyersweekly.com

VERDICTS & SETTLEMENTS

Woman hit by truck while changing flat tire

$1,150,000 Settlement

COOPER

HURLEY

Plaintiff is a 60-year-old grandmother who was struck outside her vehicle in the early morning by a commercial truck in Hampton Roads. The injuries included non-surgical fractures of the left leg, a broken bone in her neck and a broken nose. The pictures of plaintiff's swollen and bloody face made the plaintiff's claim of traumatic brain injury more understandable. CT testing also showed bleeding on the brain at the hospital emergency room. The bulk of the past medical bills of $100,000.00 were for an inpatient stay at Sentara Norfolk General Hospital and a rehabilitation facility.

Although the defense contested the traumatic brain injury as a permanent impairment, the severity of the injuries could not be denied. Plaintiff received social security as she was no longer able to return to her warehouse foreman job earning $25,000.00 annually.

Type of action:	Truck wreck/pedestrian injury
Injuries alleged:	Traumatic brain injury, non-surgical leg fractures, broken bone in her neck, broken nose
Verdict or settlement:	Settlement
Amount:	$1,150,000
Attorneys for plaintiff:	John Cooper and Jim Hurley, Norfolk

Contributory negligence allegations included that the plaintiff was changing a flat tire in the right lane of a major roadway at the time that she was hit, rather than pulling off the road, and the poor condition of the vehicle. Plaintiff's counsel's strategy included keeping the case in a favorable venue. The trucker's insomnia put the defendant in a bad light and explained his failure to see the flashers on the broken down van.

In addition to past lost wages and medical bills, the plaintiff had a work-up about future medical costs, most of which were related to in-home care for traumatic brain injury symptoms. The high-dollar life care plan was seriously challenged by the defendants. A Medicare set-aside was required.

The case settled at a lengthy mediation.

[17-T-163]

CHAPTER 20
WHAT OUR CLIENTS SAY ABOUT US

At Cooper Hurley Injury Lawyers, we treat out clients like family. We stay in touch with them after their cases have been resolved. Many of our car accident injury clients leave us favorable reviews. This is a sample of some of them.

"They are the best. I've not found a better law firm in Hampton Roads than Cooper Hurley Injury Lawyers. They are very thorough and attentive to your case as well as great in following up to ensure you're kept apprised with updates. I would highly recommend them," -**Gerry N.**

"I highly recommend Cooper Hurley Injury Lawyers. Bill O'Mara is great he kept me in the loop about what was going on with my son's case and was very compassionate. We weren't just another case. Stacy was my paralegal and she is amazing. She would answer any question I had and got back with me in a timely manner. During the final phase of everything, I know I called a lot to see what was going on, and every time she was kind, patient, and willing to help. I'm glad I had them on my side," -**Veronica E.**

"After getting into a horrible accident on the way to football practice in Norfolk I could not have chosen a better attorney than Griffin (O'Hanlon) and Cooper Hurley Injury Lawyers

.They always kept me informed about the details of my case. Highly recommend them," -**Douglas R.**

"I got into an accident in Norfolk and was referred by a family member to call Cooper Hurley Injury Lawyers - the best injury attorneys in Hampton Roads. While working with Cooper Hurley, Nicole was easy to get in contact with and always returned my calls. She kept me updated on everything about my case. I love them!" -**Shonqueta R.**

"I got into my accident in Newport News. We called up Cooper Hurley to represent and help me through all of this. I am so happy with my decision to call them! They did a great job with my situation and helping me get my settlement. Working with Nicole was great! She was so smart and understanding and helped me through this process the best way she could! Thank you very much!!" -**Ayanna L.**

"I was in an accident in Chesapeake and received a recommendation to Cooper Hurley. From the first internet experience to actual meetings this firm was on top of everything. Billy Jo was in constant contact with myself and my chiropractor. I would 100 percent recommend this firm to anyone. They are 100 percent fair and honest," -**Laurie D.**

"I thoroughly enjoyed having Cooper Hurley Injury Lawyers take care of my case after my car accident. I was hit by another vehicle the day before Christmas and was very reluctant to even sue because in a prior case the attorney involved did care about my case one bit. But I will say that at Cooper Hurley not only were they concerned throughout the process, I even got monthly updates about my case without asking for anything. They are by far the best local firm and will make sure you are compensated fairly. If ever in the future I should need another personal injury lawyer, there will be no hesitation, this firm is my go to," -**Kimberly W.**

"Cooper Hurley are AWESOME! I was in a car accident last year in November with my 2-month-old child and got injured pretty badly. Nicole was amazing, I didn't have to worry about a thing, the took care of it all for me right down to paying off my bills. My dad found Cooper Hurley online, and I couldn't be happier that he did," -**Raine F.**

"Mr. Cooper was incredibly helpful and efficient. He and his paralegal, Stephanie, were on top of my case and worked diligently to arrive at a settlement that was fair and just. I highly recommend Cooper Hurley as their professionalism and expertise are critical in a time of need," -**Hahns C.**

"I was in an accident in Virginia Beach. I called numerous lawyers and none of them would take my case. I finally called Cooper Hurley and they took my case! From the first day I met with them they made me feel comfortable. They listened to all of my concerns. My lawyer Griff O'Hanlon stayed in contact with me through the whole thing. He made sure I knew what was going on at all times. I'm so happy all the other lawyers denied taking my case. I would highly recommend calling Cooper Hurley Injury Lawyers if you have any type of accident. They are an amazing group of lawyers," -**Haley R.**

"I got into an accident in Virginia Beach and a friend of mine referred me to Cooper Hurley. It was an excellent experience. They took over everything so I could focus on the things that mattered in my life. I did not have to worry about a thing, I did not have to deal with the person who hit me, the insurance companies or the medical staff that treated me. They took care of everything," -**Bailey C.**

"After my accident heading towards the Norfolk Naval Base I called Cooper Hurley Injury Lawyers. It never felt like a job working with them, they always kept my best interests at heart. I like working with honest people and that was the best part of working with Jim and Tara. I would recommend them to anyone. Job well done," -**Gilbert G.**

CONCLUSION

It is not easy when you are hurt in a car accident that is not your fault. After the wreck, you have to worry about your injuries, getting better, property damage, and trying to deal with the defendant's insurance company. Your whole life is turned upside down from the car crash and you must be careful to protect your legal rights. We hope that the information in this book helps you to get through this difficult time.

When you are hurt in a car wreck, the most important thing is to be sure that you receive the proper medical care and get a knowledgeable and caring injury lawyer.

At Cooper Hurley Injury Lawyers, our clients trust us with helping them with all of their legal needs when they are hurt in a car accident. Please feel free to call us if you or a family member is hurt in a car crash in Virginia.

COOPER HURLEY INJURY LAWYERS

Jim Hurley, ESQ
John Cooper, ESQ
Bill O'Mara, ESQ
Griffin M. O'Hanlon, ESQ

125 St Pauls Blvd #510
Norfolk, VA 23510

757.455.0077
866.455.6657 (TOLL FREE)

WWW.COOPERHURLEY.COM

WA

Made in USA - Kendallville, IN
1079537_9781633853126
04.14.2020 1034